D0496644

DEDICATION

This book is dedicated to all of the people who refuse to settle for less, who are visionary enough to recognise the enormous opportunities available to each of us in this day and age, and who are bold enough and committed enough to do the work to make it happen.

ACKNOWLEDGEMENTS

First and foremost, I would like to thank my beautiful wife Alexna, and my children, Arya, and Hannah, for their unending support, inspiration, and love.

I would like to thank the entire team at PMW and TMD Media for their relentless commitment to push the boundaries, for their commitment to changing lives, and for their support in doing what we do. I'm proud to be a part of this family. I would also like to thank Eddie Tribe, Dylan Stewart, and Sean McIntyre for their editorial contributions and support.

My greatest thanks in writing this book are to Billy Farrell and Richard Swan, whose dedication and efforts have been exceptional. It's been my privilege and honour to work with you.

YOUR PROPERTY JUMPSTART

PAUL MCFADDEN

paulmcfaddenwealth.com

 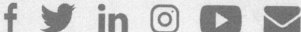

ALL RIGHTS RESERVED

EDITORIAL TEAM

Billy Farrell, Richard Swan, Sean McIntyre, Eddie Tribe, Dylan Stewart.

BOOK COVER DESIGN

TMD Media

PUBLISHER'S DISCLAIMER

CONTENTS

YOUR PROPERTY JUMPSTART

INTRODUCTION

"What the **** are you reading?" said my workmate, as he slid the van door open.

I was 22. The book was about building a successful property business.

He snatched it from my hands, waved it in front of the other tradesmen, and began to mock me.

"Paul's going to be a millionaire lads"

"Who do you think you are, Paul?"

"What do you know about property?"

The abuse went on. Needless to say, it was pretty devastating.

Truth is, I didn't realise at the time that the encounter said more about my colleague's view of the world, and his own limitations, than it did about me, but we'll come back to that. I wasn't having a good day.

I'd avoided conversation throughout the morning, and hid myself in the back of the van with my lunch and my book. Despite being 22, I was fearful that I'd never amount to much in life, and that my dreams of a brighter future wouldn't come to pass. Coming from a below average start in life, in a single parent household, I'd taken the advice of those around me and stuck in at school, graduating shortly thereafter from University with a degree in computing. I then landed a great job in I.T., with excellent prospects, but something just wasn't adding up…

Perhaps you know the feeling.

I found it difficult to accept the *status quo*, to say "Yes sir, no sir, thank you sir." To show up on time, put in the hours, and go home, only to live for the weekend and repeat the pattern the following week. It wasn't working for me. I wanted something different. I wanted more. I looked further down the line and saw my manager earning £40,000 to £50,000 per annum. He was in his late fifties. It had taken him decades of repetition, diligence, and hard work to get there, and it was as high as he was going.

Despite the unsolicited advice from those around me, I left my job in I.T. and set upon my first entrepreneurial pursuit. To cut a long story short, not long after starting, amidst the words of "I told you so," and the jeers and criticism of those around me, I failed, very publicly, and very miserably. Now here I was, a short time later, working as a general labourer, enduring the abuse of my colleagues.

It was tempting to let the encounter get the better of me, to remind myself that I lived in a housing estate in the South-side of Glasgow, that I had no money, no credit, no experience, and no knowledge of property or business. It was tempting to focus on where I'd come from, as well as my current circumstances.

But this time, something snapped.

I took a good hard look at my reality, and decided I'd had enough.

Whatever attracted you to this book, and wherever you are in life, I want you to know something. If a thing is humanly possible, it's within your reach. If other people, from similar backgrounds to your own, have achieved their goals, then why not you? These are the thoughts that ran through my mind, and forced me back into the world of property and business, this time, with a burning desire and a drive that refused to accept failure. No matter how many times I fell, I would always stand back up. No matter how many times I was mocked or verbally abused, I'd continue forward.

To say it was smooth sailing would be a lie. It was difficult. Most people would have given up when faced with the hurdles I was forced to overcome.

But I was blind to any other outcome than absolute success. I wanted more from life, I wanted to change my circumstances, and I desperately wanted to get out of the rat race and become the best possible version of myself.

It's taken me 11 years to get to where I am today, to be living a life beyond my wildest aspirations…

Living on Scotland's most expensive residential street, marrying my beautiful wife Alexna, spending half the year in our home in Costa Rica, giving our daughters every opportunity in life that I never had, to owning and operating multiple companies in the property world and various other industries, including our development company, our property investment fund, our property training academy, our building company and more…

My life is pretty damn awesome. I live a life of security and freedom, and most importantly fulfilment.

Now, I don't say this to impress. That's not my style.

I say this to enlighten you, that if this dyslexic lad from Glasgow, with every possible excuse, reason, and justification not to succeed in anything other than a low-end position in the rat race, can do this, then why not you?

Here's the best part...

It took me 11 years to stand where I stand today.

It doesn't have to take you 11 years to do the same.

Upon deciding I would pursue my fortunes in property, I sold my possessions to raise funds to pay for my education. I took multiple training courses. I read book after book after book. I worked with some phenomenal mentors, and endured some harsh lessons through others. I risked it all, borrowed money, 'maxed-out' credit cards, and put myself in a dangerous financial position, in order to learn everything that I had to know about property and business; and thankfully, it was worth the investment.

What you have in your hands, is the guide I wish I had available when I first started.

This book, *Your Property Jumpstart* ™, is not only a culmination of my education, but more importantly, a direct reflection and culmination of 11 years of experience; both the failures, and the successes. This book is my journey of what works, and what has stood the test of time in property, to allow not only myself, but many of the students in our *Property Protege* ™ programme, to go full-time in property, to build six-figure businesses, to create seven-figure property portfolios, and to ultimately live the life they desired.

Now, I realise that all of this can come across as motivational hype, but results don't lie. We are a deal-doing company first, and an education company second. We live and breathe property. It's what we do, each and every day; and through this book and our *Property Protege Intensive*, we enjoy the opportunity to support, mentor, and many times work directly with those who follow suit.

For those who do the work, the results will follow.

It's that simple.

You can make money, or you can make excuses, but you can't make both.

PROPERTY CYCLES

When I first started in property, we were in pre-recession. I'd gone into this whole new world, and as I was still learning, the glory days were coming to an end. Had I gone in a few years earlier, I'd likely have ended up making the same mistakes I witnessed others making. It was an upward market. Everyone and anyone was involved. You didn't need money. Banks and lenders were giving it away. People were getting 120% funding, sub-prime mortgages were being touted as the next best thing with mortgage brokers self-certifying mortgages without carrying out proper checks. It was crazy.

The strategy primarily being taught and followed, was to buy, and then refinance, year after year, jumping from lender to lender. Whilst this was considered a good strategy in an upward market, it wasn't a sensible way to invest. It was a highly flawed and reckless strategy, but almost everyone was blind to it and continued to over-leverage, not thinking of the potential consequences.

What I could plainly see, was the Wild West, and what made more sense to me, based on what I'd been learning, my own insights, and good old common sense, was to buy right; to buy below market value, or to buy where I knew I could add value, or both. I began to realise that if a property was bought right, and was approached with thorough due diligence and professionalism, then a savvy investor could pull their funds out in a short space of time, giving them an infinite return without the need to continue to refinance any more than once.

Having just entered into the property market I started to notice a gradual decline in the pattern that I'd studied in that very book in the back of the work van. I started to see house prices fall. At first it was gradual and a lot of the apparent professional investors around me were in denial and continued to buy without a care in the world.

And then, in late 2008, the market crashed.

What was once an upward market; became a spiralling downward market.

Many of the people involved in property, who'd been over-enthusiastic and amateur in their approach, were taken out of the game.

People began losing jobs, banks recalled loans, negative equity became prevalent, people had fire-sales on their portfolios, and the market went into a frenzy of selling. As a result, house prices dropped, there was more stock than buyers, finance became harder and harder to obtain, and the idea of adding value and selling was no longer a viable strategy, because nobody was buying. Of course, none of this mattered much to those who'd bought right, or cashed in, through intelligent investing and intelligent business.

For those who'd been savvy, the downward market was the perfect opportunity to build a portfolio. The market was awash with stock, properties were being sold at heavier discounts, the number of motivated sellers was off the charts, and for those who could get the finance, this was the perfect opportunity to buy right.

Before the recession hit, I had purchased my first buy-to-let property. I'd been patient, I'd been observing and studying the market, seeing the early signs of sellers becoming motivated, and I purchased my first property that I'd ever bought at a discount at 15% below market value, which I thought was excellent at the time. My second purchase was for my own home however this time emotion got the better of me and we paid top price for it. Not ideal, as we entered into the recession and what seemed like overnight we were in negative equity on our home and my buy-to-let property dropped by around 15% in value.

This is where my credit started to take a massive hit as I had increased my overdrafts, taken out loans and credit cards to fund my education and to help raise the deposits to fund my first two property purchases. It was time to get serious and play this game the right way.

I really got started at a time when most people were avoiding the property market, fearful of a further decline. Many were struggling, and panicking. I had already purchased a couple of properties and had encountered first-hand how quickly my own property values dropped, but I knew that with the right level of knowledge, the correct due diligence, and the proper mindset and work ethic, that I could succeed in property.

This is where I started to focus on building wealth for others, primarily through sourcing deals and selling them to other investors. Very quickly I had amassed the funds and knowledge to begin aggressively building my own portfolio and property business.

I worked with joint venture partners when my ability to get mortgages came to a halt.

I continued to sell deals, that didn't fit my own criteria, to other investors.

I also continued to help other investors to buy, add value, and sell, as an equal partner.

I cleaned up and kicked ass.

What's the point of all of this?

It doesn't matter whether it's an upward market, a downward market, or a plateauing market. It doesn't matter if there's a Brexit, a meltdown, or Independence...

RIGHT NOW IS THE PERFECT TIME

The fact is, whether you're reading this in 2018, or 2038, if you're savvy in your approach, if you properly conduct your due diligence, if you follow the eight key fundamentals detailed in this book, and you buy right, or help others to do the same, then there's a world of opportunity available to you.

If you buy a property, add value, and sell it, you make substantially more, right?

If you help others do the same, if you're not in a position to do the deal yourself, then you have the complimentary skills that give you an equal or negotiable place in the investment, right?

Whatever the market, if you're smart about it, you'll win.

There are multiple strategies available to you.

A true professional should be making money, whatever the market conditions; knowing when to pivot and what strategy to focus on next. What is covered in this book will allow you to operate and thrive in any market condition.

That's why you're here, right?

Because you want to win, and you want to win big?

Because you want to insulate yourself from the downside, whilst enjoying an unlimited upside?

Because you want to learn how to succeed in property whether you have the funds or not?

Let me tell you straight...

You're in the right place.

This book is not light reading.

This book will challenge you.

This book will push you.

But for those of you willing to stay the course, this book will help you change your life.

I'm going to walk you through a series of steps before bringing it all together with your WAR PLAN.

We're going to start with the property millionaire mindset. If all you learn from this book are a handful of strategies, but you fail to become the person who can implement them, then all you'll have is a guide for making the same amount of money you're already making. Why is it that someone can come into money overnight, and lose it, whereas someone who has amassed financial wealth can lose it, and build it back again? It all comes down to mindset. This is the most important element of *Your Property Jumpstart* ™. We must become the kind of person who can make it happen, and raise our unconscious upper limits on wealth.

We'll then move into the foundations, where we discuss the five reasons why property is your number one vehicle for the life and business you desire. We'll discuss whether you need money or not, knowing and committing to your strategy, finding the deals, mastering the figures, and the entire property purchase process, including what happens after you buy. We'll then discuss and break down property jargon, as I become your translator in a world full of buzz words and acronyms.

In Chapter three, we'll discuss the fundamentals and your property power team. We'll discuss each of the eight key fundamentals for building a successful and long-lasting property business, before discussing each of the key players in your property power team, which forms the back bone of your property business.

In Chapter four, we'll discuss Goldmine Area research, and due diligence. We'll discuss the importance of knowing your target area inside out, how to determine where your target area should be, and how to be the ultimate expert in knowing your patch, as well as understanding how to conduct thorough due diligence, in order to know when a deal is a deal, and when it's not.

In Chapter five, after laying the foundations, the key fundamentals, understanding our target area, and knowing what a deal should look like, we move into investment strategies, sharing multiple case studies, pulling deals apart, looking at each opportunity as a potential deal to add to a portfolio, or to buy-to-flip. This section of the book, having been built on the content preceding it, will open your eyes, blow your mind, and give you the drive you want, coupled with the knowledge and strategies to make it happen.

In Chapter six, we'll discuss my favourite subject, Property Trading and Deal Packaging. This is how I made my money. When I started, I had no funds, no credit, no network, and no perceived chance. What I did instead, was focus on how I could help others through the knowledge I'd gathered. I began to source the deals on one hand, whilst finding the buyers on the other. I'd sit in the middle, and through what you're going to learn in this section of the book, began making upwards of £7,000 per trade, without buying, or selling property. This is the core strategy we begin with at *Property Protege* ™, as it's without doubt the easiest and fastest way to create serious cashflow to kickstart and launch your property business.

In Chapter seven, we're going to dig into the subject of raising finance. We'll discuss how your mindset around raising finance is more important than your abilities or perceived abilities. We'll talk about how to find preferred investors who are only too willing to give you money. We'll talk about how to leverage debt and why debt is a positive thing when invested the right way. We'll break down several myths around raising finance. We'll discuss traditional funding, non-traditional funding, commercial funding and private funding. In this section of the book, as with every other section, your eyes will be truly open to what's possible.

In Chapter eight, we're going to explore the power of joint ventures (JV's), the benefits and the risks, how to plan a successful JV, how to choose your JV partners, how to secure your interests, and how to build upon your property business, again, without the funds, the credit, and the ability to get mortgages.

In Chapter nine, we're going to discuss property deal sourcing. Let's face it, if you have no deals, then you have no income and no business. In this chapter, I am going to share with you, step by step, what we've been doing over the past 11 years to source unlimited amounts of deals. We'll break down and discuss each step of the deal sourcing process, what works, what doesn't work, and what I would do if starting again today.

In Chapter ten, we'll discuss negotiation and making offers. To this point in the book, you'll have learned how to find the deals, raise the funds, sell the deals, know when a deal is a deal, and so on. Now, you'll learn how to negotiate like a professional, in order to achieve the best win win outcome for yourself, and the seller.

In Chapter eleven, we bring it all home, with your property war plan, discussing exactly what to do, having gained the knowledge you're going to gain in this book.

Once again, this is the guide I wish I had when I started in property.

Follow this guide.
Commit to it.
Get obsessed about it.
Don't overcomplicate it.
Keep it simple.
Do the work.
And enjoy the results.
You're in for one hell of a ride. Let's get started…

paulmcfadden.com

INTRODUCTION

CHAPTER ONE:
THE PROPERTY MILLIONAIRE MINDSET

"Show me the money…"

That's why you're here, right? To learn about property investment?

To learn strategies such as buy-to-let, buy-to-flip, and packaging deals to trade? To learn the various strategies available to you? To learn how to find the deals and raise funds to bring them to life?

Great. We can walk you through it.

But first, we must address the one common denominator that will either propel you to the heights of success or will bring a swift close to all progress and ambition.

The biggest challenge you have, and the biggest problem you're going to have, is you.

At our signature Property Protege ™ Intensive, we spend the first morning of the workshop on mindset. If time and circumstance allowed it, we'd extend the event by several days and spend the majority of our time on mindset.

Why? Because your mind is the number one thing that makes the biggest difference.

The problem is rarely one of raising finance, sourcing deals or investment strategies. The problem is how you choose to approach the day-to-day ups-and-downs of business. The problem is with your wealth thermostat and personal capacity. The problem is with your attitude towards problems. The problem is with your approach to personal responsibility, vision, attitude, and focus. Ultimately and overall, your mindset.

If we were to take each person reading this and extend an invite to a gathering in 12-months from now, some people would have left full-time employment, created financial freedom, and achieved their own personal ambitions. On the flip side, other people just wouldn't show up, some would come for the banter, and some would have a fantastic list of justifiable reasons for why it didn't or couldn't happen for them.

In our experience of working with thousands of investors and property deal traders, both new and experienced, over the past decade, you can make money, or you can make excuses, but you can't make both. You can have reasons, or results, but if you lack results, then chances are you'll have a great list of reasons for why it didn't happen.

And in our experience, for every obstacle that stands in a person's way, there's at least one example of someone else who has faced similar, or even more difficult challenges, and yet achieved success regardless.

There's a path in front of you.

There are obstacles, pitfalls, challenges, and dangers; all there to slow you down.

Further down the path however, are those who have successfully navigated the terrain and who now stand where you hope to one day stand. They're cheering you on. They're giving you the road map and a detailed guide on how to get there, minus the level of difficulty that they themselves pushed through. They're showing you how to do it faster, and with less cuts and bruises. They're showing you the way.

The question is, will you take the advice and run with it? Or will you learn the hard way?

Allow me to be your guide.

It all starts with your mindset.

IF A THING IS HUMANLY POSSIBLE, CONSIDER IT WITHIN REACH

No matter your past, you have a spotless future.

Whatever happened before you came to read this book, consider it behind you. What happens from this point forward, is an entirely different story, and you now possess a blank canvas upon which to paint.

Growing up as I did, I remember passively and experientially learning about money from those around me. Popular phrases in our environment included, "money doesn't grow on trees", "rich people must have ripped-off or stepped on other people", "making money is not for people like us", "it takes money to make money", and so on.

Knowing nothing of life other than what I learned from those around me, I began to find myself living in accordance with such beliefs. Without knowing the cause, this led to years of frustration. I wanted more from life. I wanted to know why others could achieve the kind of life that I could only dream of, while I was stuck firmly in my designated place in the world. From seeing my friends with the newest clothing or games as a child, to witnessing successful people living a life I could only imagine as an adult. But hey, making money wasn't for people like me...

Until one day, I found myself reading an article by Tony Robbins, one of the world's leading voices in personal development, where Tony told his own story which shared many similarities with my own. The difference being, Tony had woken up and broken through.

Tony shared how his life had changed when he adopted one singular belief, that "If a thing is humanly possible, consider it to be within your reach."

In an instant, reading Tony's words, I felt my vision expand. I began to feel excited and nervous simultaneously. My entire perspective began to shift, and in that moment, a whole new world of possibility, potential, and opportunity, opened up to me.

If a thing is possible, consider it within reach.

Is it possible to become a billionaire? Yes. Many have done it. It's a big ask, but it's still possible. Is it possible to become an astronaut? Yes. Many have done it. Equally, a big ask, but still possible, particularly in this day and age of modern space exploration and the onset of commercial space flights.

Is it possible to become a millionaire? I asked myself. My own end desire at the time. The answer was not only an unquestionable yes, but when I read the statistics that 10 million others had achieved it (now in 2018 that number is 15 million), and 90% of the 10 million people were first generation rich, I decided in that moment that I would join them.

I knew it was possible, and I was going to make it happen.

And now I extend the same challenge to you.

YOUR WEALTH THERMOSTAT

Here's the deal. Your income can only grow to the extent that you do.

There are people with rich mindsets and there are people with poverty mindsets.

If you took a rich person's money away, chances are they'd find a way to earn it back. If you gave money to a person with a poverty mindset, chances are they'd end up worse off (statistically speaking).

Whether you consider yourself someone with a rich mindset, or a poverty mindset, each of us has our income range; our own unconscious limits on wealth; a level of comfort that we identify with.

I remember a recent trip to Vegas; spending some time with a group of young entrepreneurs. One of them made a statement that struck me. He said, "I just can't imagine earning any less than £50,000 per month." This was a clear measure of his own unconscious limits. He couldn't imagine earning any less than his £50,000 monthly income, and as expected, he wasn't earning much more than that either.

Some people can't imagine earning any less than £2,000, or £3,000 per month. If they ever lost their income, they'd find a way of making that same number or just a little bit more, just as the chap in Vegas would have found a way to replace his own £50,000 per month if anything ever happened. Different mindsets; different ideas of what's possible. We have our lower-end figure, and a top-end figure that we rarely extend beyond. Both just a few short numbers apart from the other.

Let's delve into this…

Imagine for a moment, a thermostat in the room.

When it gets too hot, what happens?

The air conditioning kicks-in and brings the room back to set point; the comfort zone.

In the same way, when it gets too hot financially, or even when the idea kicks-in for something outside of your comfort zone, your own programming and conditioning will step in and create mental havoc.

So how do we raise the set-point, fast?

How do we raise our own limits?

Firstly, we have to take your temperature.

So let me ask you…

- How much money could you lose right now without losing your mind?
- What's the average worth of your five closest friends?
- What did you learn about money growing up?
- What are you feeding yourself mentally day-to-day?
- What's been your average bank balance over the past three months to three years?
- Could you be playing a more aggressive game?

I'm never surprised these days when people tell me, "I'm going to be a millionaire," yet if they lost £50 they'd lose their minds, or others who still hang onto beliefs such as "Money isn't for people like us," or people who spend the money they get, because it's how they've always seen it done, or who listen to the news on the radio, instead of feeding their minds with inspirational educational audiobooks or podcasts, or people who talk about money and abundance, but focus on lack and limitation.

Reality doesn't lie. Your outer world is a direct reflection of your inner world.

Don't like the fruits? Change the roots.

Remember, the past does not equal the future, and if a thing is humanly possible, if many other people have made it happen, then consider it within reach.

So how do we change the roots?

REPROGRAMMING THE WEALTH THERMOSTAT

Let's share a few ideas…

Surround yourself with people who are on the same journey, or more importantly, those who are further ahead.

Birds of a feather flock together. Ever notice how people with similar interests tend to spend time with one another? Sounds obvious right? Car enthusiasts hang around other car enthusiasts. Gym fanatics hang around with other gym fanatics. Football fans hang around with other football fans. As we said, it sounds obvious, but let me ask you, who are you spending time with? What's the level of conversation you're taking in? Are you spending time with people who talk about football, nights out with an excess of alcohol, the latest episode of whatever trash TV is current and popular, or general day-to-day chat? Or are you spending time with people who inspire you, drive you, hold you to a higher standard, and keep you moving forward? When the conversation changes, so do the results. When the company changes, so too does your expanded network, and new doors begin to open.

When you spend time with people who talk about bigger numbers, bigger deals, bigger opportunities and smarter business, you'll find your own belief in what's possible, and your own idea of what's acceptable and achievable dramatically increase. You won't settle for less.

Test drive the car and view the dream home…

First of all, test driving powerful or dream cars, and visiting dream homes, will be a heck of a lot of fun, but there are several reasons I suggest you do this. The first time I visited a £1m+ home, I was in awe. I went in, wandered around, and imagined living there. I viewed a showhome so I'd have unaccompanied time to explore. When I went back to my own home, it just felt small and unfulfilling. I'd had a taste of the big life, and I wanted more. Similarly, the car. I remember test driving a new Bentley, after parking my old BMW M3 in the Bentley car park. My car had felt awesome before I went in, but afterwards, I was embarrassed to drive it. Now, if this sounds a little extreme, I want you to understand the logic. It's not about the car, nor is it about the house. It's about continually sending messages to your brain that you will not settle for a lower standard of living. It's about letting every part of you know, that this is the new standard for your life, and pulling together the internal drive and resources to make it happen. Oh, and it's fun, did I mention that?

Commit to personal growth…

Stop listening to the radio. Stop watching the news. Stop listening to other people bitch and moan about their lives. Change the channel. Start listening to positive, educational, inspirational and motivational podcasts and audiobooks. Replace the newspaper with Success Magazine. Unfollow everyone on Facebook, and then refollow people you care about, and actively follow pages that share content, images and videos on things that match the new upgraded quality of life you desire. Become learner. Don't read 1,000 books once. Read a handful of books hundred times if you must. Master specific content. For example, you c read this book once, and then move on to the next property book, or yo could make it your mission to know this content like the back of your hand, to make it second nature to you. One of these approaches will help you become wealthy. The other, will make you a great contestant on The Chase.

Join us at Property Protege ™

Hey, it goes without saying. What better way to get around the right people, access the right mentorship, and get the best education, than to join us on our flagship Property Protege ™ programme; that is of course if you like what you're reading throughout this book and you resonate with us. The fact is, we turn away more people than we accept, because we will accept nothing less than a focused group of committed individuals, driven to change their lives. The entry level 'musts' include: ambition; drive; attitude; and a vision for a better life. There's no purposeless negativity allowed. We focus on solutions, and we help one another succeed. You still have to do the work, but you'll have the education, the support, the backing, the team, the resources, and everything else you'll need, right at your fingertips.

Technically, you can't fully reprogram yourself…

What we can do, is consistently condition ourselves, which in turn helps us become the version of ourselves that we're after, whilst making it easier to stay there with low maintenance. The learning, the education, the expansion of vision, and the drive; it never ends. It will change your life.

CLARIFY YOUR RICH VISION

So what does rich look like to you?

I don't just mean fancy cars, big houses and designer clothing.

What truly lights you up?

What would the perfect day look like? Where would you wake up? Who would you wake up beside? How would you spend your time? Who would you spend your time with? What physical condition would you be in?

routine look like? What would you do for personal

 is, many of the things that constitute a rich vision,

we just don't do them. Hopefully, you change that,

re matters. Achievement and fulfilment are two

You can pursue fulfilment through 'blissing out' all day whilst making no money, or you can strive for achievement whilst failing to enjoy the simple things that make you truly come alive. Or, you can be intelligent and balance both.

So what does your rich vision look like? What do you want to be, do, and have? Why are you doing what you're doing? How do you want to contribute? What does your idea of a rich day look like?

You get the idea.

Get it written down.

You can't score unless you know where the goals are.

Take the time to gain clarity on what you want and why, and then visualise it daily, affirm it daily, obsess over it daily, live it daily, breathe it daily, and hunt it, daily.

Property is the vehicle.

HAVE A RUTHLESS COMMITMENT TO YOUR GOALS

Now that we've established that it's possible.

And we've committed to raising our unconscious upper-limits on wealth.

And we've clarified our rich vision.

Let's talk about commitment, and what that looks like.

When I first started down the path of personal development, there was a bookshelf in Waterstones dedicated to what was then known as pop psychology, and business. Nowadays, you have entire floors dedicated to both subjects. It's popular to want to be in business. Many people share the dream, but the real question is, who's prepared to put in the work to make it happen?

To me, commitment is like pregnancy. You're either pregnant or you're not. There's no in-between. You're not pregnant during working hours, followed by a few hours off, later that day.

Commitment to your goals first requires knowing what you're going after, which we've discussed. It then requires doing whatever it takes, legally, morally, and ethically to get there.

Regularly, people tell me, "Paul, I'll do whatever it takes…"

"…as long as I don't have to travel to Glasgow."
"…as long as I don't have to work nights."
"…as long as I don't have to network."
"…as long as I don't have to raise funds."
"…as long as I don't have to do any public speaking."
"…as long as I don't have to pay anything."

I hate to break it to you, but that's not whatever it takes.

Whatever it takes, means, 'whatever-it-fricken-takes!'

Too many people aren't willing to do whatever it takes. They make success conditional on various criteria, and then wonder why it's not happening for them.

When high performance people set an outcome, they don't procrastinate on it. They don't overthink it. They don't put limitation or condition in their way. They aggressively charge after it, and mow down anything and anyone that attempts to stop them. They do whatever it takes.

In business, you can make money or you can make excuses, but you can't make both. If you are truly willing to go after it, then there are no excuses, it's a simple war path with the occasional shift in strategy until the outcome is met. For every excuse you have as to why things didn't work out for you, or can't work out for you, there are countless other people who faced more difficult circumstances and situations, and still came out on top.

TAKE 100% RESPONSIBILITY FOR YOUR LIFE

I remember the day I realised I'd been a victim.

I was feeling frustrated with a joint venture partner who I believed wasn't pulling their weight. I arranged to meet with him, with grand plans on how I'd sort him out. Fat chance. The moment I sat down, he laid into me, and pointed out how I was a victim. Everything else was always at fault. It was never on me; it was always down to something or someone else. I listened, quietly, and then left. My grand ideas on how I was going to handle him were out the window, and I went home to do some thinking.

Could it really be that I was a victim?

I decided to do some reading online and came to three conclusions that sum up the word victim.

Blame. Complain. Justify.

Whenever I found myself either blaming, complaining, or justifying, I wasn't in a position of power. If life was happening 'to me', rather than 'for me' or 'by me' then I was a passenger, and had little to no control over whatever was going on. It stung. It hit me hard. But it was true. I'd gone in, blaming the other person for my own lack of results, without thinking about the work he'd been doing or the effort he'd been putting in. In my mind, it was his fault that we weren't moving forward.

When I discovered the three actions of victims, I decided that the exact opposite of being on the receiving end was to take 100% responsibility for my life, my business and my results. Even if things went horribly wrong, my first question would be, "How did I allow this to happen?" or "How did I create this?" or "How did I attract this?" It would never be from a place of victimhood, but from a place of strength, because once I established how I allowed something to happen, I'd learn a lesson, before getting back in the driver's seat and deciding how to push forward.

In your property business things are going to go wrong. Rather than wishing it wasn't the case, I'd recommend you expect it and treat it as part of the game, which it is. People will let you down, people will mislead you, people will pull out on deals, people will tell you they have funds, and they don't. Shit will hit the fan, and when it does, your focus must be "How did I let it happen?" followed by: "What must change, and what can I do right now to change it and drive us forward?" Do this, and you'll keep moving forward. Get caught up in the blame game and you'll end up bitter, frustrated, and stuck.

SEEK OUT THE NEW NORMAL

I want you to think about the job you're in, or the business you're in…

When you first began, were there things you didn't know or understand? Was some of it a little scary? Were there elements that stretched you, or made you feel uncomfortable?

And after a while, did those things become second nature; the new normal?

Whenever we do something for the first time, particularly if we perceive it to be a stretch, it's going to feel uncomfortable. But very quickly, it just becomes who we are. We don't have to think about it. It's like driving a car. On your first lesson you have no idea what you're doing, and you had no idea there were so many things to think about and take into account. And yet, if you're a driver nowadays, you just cruise along comfortably and everything flows as it should, right?

Well, you're now stepping into the property game, and you're going to come up against it. The first time you raise finance will be a stretch, the first time you do a financial presentation will be a stretch, the first time you negotiate with a seller will be a stretch, and the first time you spend money on marketing will be a stretch. Many aspects of what you're going to do will be uncomfortable, but here's where so many people go wrong…

They think the fact that it's uncomfortable is some sort of justification that this game just isn't for them; that making money isn't for people like them. That this property stuff is better left to the professionals; that they're kidding themselves on. The reality is, making money and running a property business, are just a series of skillsets that are learned and developed over time. The first time you step into the fire, you're going to feel the heat. Soon, after being in there a few times, it starts to become normal. Allow yourself to be uncomfortable and to feel the heat, because if you do, you'll get to the other side, and it'll be a breeze.

Big problems become little, when you become bigger.

FOCUS FOCUS FOCUS

Ever heard of shiny object syndrome? No? I'll bet you've fallen for it though.

Shiny object syndrome takes people out of the game.

You're charging down the path, you're having a difficult moment, and then someone or something pops up to show you an easier way. You know it's a distraction. You know you should stay focused, but it's difficult. You want the easy route, and it's too damn appealing not to have a look.

In property, it's like this. You've bought this book called *Your Property Jumpstart* ™. You may even have applied for and been accepted on

Property Protege ™. You're focused on your strategy, when suddenly, a Facebook ad pops up, promising that if you just invest in the latest crypto currency, you can make a six-figure income from a beach in the Bahamas, working 20 minutes per day.

There's a reason why race horses wear blinders. It's to stop them from seeing what's going on to their side and behind them. It's to stop them from becoming distracted or panicked. Their focus is on what's ahead, and their mission is full frontal assault. Take a leaf from the horse's book. Put the blinders on. Do your prep work in advance of the race you're about to run, which you're essentially doing here, and then focus on the road ahead.

When we discuss the subject of focus at Property Protege ™, we generally show a picture of a mountain. We say, "This is my mountain. It's not going to be easy, but I've prepared, I've packed my kit, I have every essential resource with me, I have my guide, and despite knowing that there will be challenging moments, I WILL stand atop this mountain and plant my flag." At this point, your friend tells you there's an easier smaller climb nearby, and the views are ten times better. Put those blinders back on. You've set your course, you've committed, now start the climb, and do not stop until you reach the top.

THE GOOD OPINION OF OTHER PEOPLE

One of the biggest killers of dreams is the need to be a people pleaser.

It's easier to say yes when we want to say no.

It's easier not to rock the boat, than take a stand.

There's a story, apocryphal or not, about a well-known spiritual teacher who was about to give a speech to 10,000 people. The subject matter was controversial. As the teacher prepared to take the stage, one of his aides asked him, "Aren't you afraid of what they'll think?" To which he replied, "There are 10,000 sets of upbringings, conditioning, life experiences, values, beliefs and backgrounds out there. Should I be concerned about each individual one? Or the collective whole?"

When you step up and begin to push forward on your dreams and ambitions, there will be pushback from people who know you. You'll have some who mean well; who don't want to see you get hurt. You'll have others who base your possibilities on their own failures and limitations.

12

You'll have some who think they know how property works, who challenge the very idea of it, and you'll have some others who just aren't very supportive or kind.

It doesn't matter who pushes back. The fact is, when you step outside your comfort zone, you automatically stretch the comfort zones of the people around you. You, being in your usual place, allows others to feel safe. It's their version of normal. Since you can't change that, you simply have to accept it.

Believe me, I've been there.

When I first started in property, I'd walk into a family gathering and have people shout, "There's Paul the Millionaire" to mock me, clearly. I had childhood friends call and leave prank voicemails, making a fool of me. A few, who I thought were friends, asked me if I thought I was better than them, and began to change their attitudes towards me, simply because I was spending more time learning and working, than playing football, talking about girls, and getting drunk at the weekend. I had work colleagues rip me to shreds and criticise my every comment. One particular day, as I was reading a book about building wealth through property, a colleague threw open the side door of the van that I was having my break inside, and grabbed the book. He then proceeded to loudly read statements from the book to the other workmen. It was pretty damn embarrassing, and could have been a major setback if I'd allowed it to be.

Don't think you're exempt from this kind of thing. It's going to happen.

And then there's the pushback from people you don't know on social media and elsewhere.

There's too much noise in the world.

You have one life. Live it. Do what you want with it.

If we think about the likes of Barrack Obama, or Donald Trump; these men were, and are, hated or disliked by over a third of their countrymen. Imagine walking into your place of work tomorrow and almost half of the workforce couldn't stand the sight of you, and they were vocal in their distaste. How would you feel about your working day? Well, I guess that's why there aren't many Obamas or Trumps in the world.

The turtle only moves forward when he sticks his neck out.

The point, he has to stick his neck out.

But what about your partner or close family?

Here's my advice: don't talk business with family.

Unless your uncle or your dad or your brother have built substantial wealth through property, they'll have much less for you to hear than the knowledge you're gaining in this book. Take advice from those who've walked the path before you. Avoid conversations about business where possible with family. It's just not worth the aggravation or the strain on relationships.

As for your partner, sometimes people get a little pushback from their other half. This is normal. There's an element of fear involved. They may be worried about you. They may be worried for themselves because you have a new direction or lease of life. Here's the best remedy I've found: put money on the table. Less talk, more action. Demonstrate the results, without what you're doing having too much of an impact on your personal life, and show them what you can do. On the same note, try not to share too many negatives with your partner. Many people wonder why their partners are worried, but never equate it to the fact that all they do is talk about how stressful and tough it is. Is it any wonder they're panicking? Instead, take your loved ones into a positive environment, and share the vision; your deepest reasons for doing what you're doing, and your desired outcome for a better life for all involved. If they don't understand you, they can't back you.

Here's the funniest thing about the good opinion of others...when you start to make it big, all of the voices who doubted you, will tell you they always had your back.

PROPERTY SPECIFIC MINDSET ESSENTIALS

Isn't it interesting, that in almost the full first chapter of a property book, we've spoken very little about property? Remember, you can learn how to do the deals, but if you don't change your mindset first, all you'll learn are a handful of strategies to earn what you're already capable of earning right now. We must radically transform our mindsets daily and commit to never ending growth in this area. Let's cover a few important points as they relate to property specifically...

A property business is not a hobby. Don't treat it like one. This is a business. Even if you're starting part-time, treat it as a business. File your paperwork, look after your paper trail, work the numbers, keep proper

books and accounting, conduct thorough due diligence, and
element of the business from marketing to prospecting to facil
you treat it like a hobby, you'll have hobby income. If you treat
business, watch how fast things begin to move.

Don't sweat the small stuff, and remember, it's all small stuff. We
must go in with the attitude that we're going to do hundreds of deals. If
you get caught up or emotionally invested in a specific deal, or you find
yourself painting or decorating or rewiring a property, you're doing it
wrong. There is no emotion here. Just because you're a plasterer by trade,
doesn't mean you should be plastering your renovation projects and
enlisting your family to help. Your numbers, which we'll discuss, should
factor in the labour, and you should be focused on finding the next deal and
securing the funds to make it happen. You are the conductor of the
orchestra; at no point are you playing the instruments.

Get your first deal done. You can intellectually understand the
process, but you don't truly know it, until you've cut your teeth and gone
through it. There's no point waiting for the perfect deal. The perfect deal
only shows itself when you're in the game. If you're too busy waiting, then
chances are, you wouldn't even know what perfect looked like, nor would
you be prepared when it came along.

Ideal circumstances will never come. Ideal is a dream. The right
timing is a fantasy. If you put it off for another six months because you're
facing challenges in your life, then all you're going to do is arrive in six
months time with a fresh batch of challenges. Start now; get perfect later.

WHO DO YOU NEED TO BECOME?

One of my favourite stories is of Darren Hardy; former editor of Success
magazine. Darren tells of how he wrote several pages describing his perfect
woman. He went into great detail on every aspect of what this woman
looked like, talked like, laughed like, and what she enjoyed to drink as well
as what she enjoyed eating, where she liked to shop, and what she
appreciated culturally. He went deep on this.

Darren then asked his own mentor, "Ok, where do I find her?"
To which he replied...

't where you find her. The question is who do you
o be worthy of such a woman? Who do you have
one of that calibre?"

ren, in your property business, the question isn't
nance?" or "How do you secure the deals?" or
sellers or investors to take you seriously?"

'Who do you have to become, in order to be
...tny of finance, of deals, and of the respect of others?"

Don't be scared off by this. When I started, I was bordering my late teens and early twenties. I looked around 12 years old. When I spoke, it was by no means polished. I have a picture of myself presenting at The Scottish Property Meet, which I started and which grew to become the country's largest property networking event, but in the picture, my shirt was hanging out. I was very rough around the edges. However, I knew what I was talking about. I learned the game inside out. I stopped hanging around with certain people, and changed my peer group. I was no longer seen as someone who bitched or moaned or brought any level of negativity to the table. I was going somewhere, and the fact is, people follow people who are going somewhere. Whoever you are right now, think about how other people see you. Think about what you're putting out on social media and the picture that paints. Think about how you speak when you're in company. Think about how you dress when you're out and about. Realise something: you are always on stage, whether you like it or not. Use this to your advantage and determine how other people see you. Be very conscious about this. It will serve you.

As we bring this chapter to a close, let me leave you with a thought…

If you will do, for the next 1 to 4 years, what no one else will do…

Then you can have, for the rest of your life, what no one else can have.

It'll happen as fast or slow as you choose, but if you do what no one else is prepared to, or is willing to, then watch how fast you can live a life that others can only dream of.

And then smile, when you're called an overnight success, or lucky.

Ok, we've covered some of the core elements of the property millionaire mindset. Now, let's start talking property. We're going to start with the foundations and fundamentals. This is the solid ground you're going to build your empire upon. Let nothing escape your grasp. Go in with eyes wide open and soak up every word. Not one thing has been said without purpose. Learn it, absorb it, and use it.

BONUS CONTENT

Visit YourPropertyJumpstart.com/bonus
for your secret bonus chapter, the Protege Deal Calculator,
and additional content and resources to support you
on your property journey

CHAPTER 2:
THE FOUNDATIONS

The fact that you're reading this book goes a long way to suggest that you already know property is a powerful vehicle for financial success. Allow me to share our five favourite reasons, why we believe property is your number one vehicle towards the life and business you desire.

CAPITAL GROWTH

There are three ways you can benefit from capital growth…

• Capital growth from property prices increasing over time.
• Capital growth from buying at a price below the market value.
• Capital growth by adding value through renovating the property.

Let's address each in turn.

When most people think about property, there's a general idea that a property investor will buy a property, rent the property to tenants, and enjoy the rental income whilst the property increases in value over time. This is known as a buy-to-let (BTL) strategy, and whilst there are many advanced forms of buy-to-let or buy-and-hold strategies, we'll keep it simple for now, as we build up your understanding.

Statistically speaking, it's been said that a property will double in value every ten years. This certainly hasn't been the case in the past decade (at the time of writing) after emerging from the Global Recession.

However, travel back two hundred years until now, and you'll find the pattern more accurate and balanced over time. Whether property doubles in value in the next ten years or not, it will still increase in value, and providing you buy 'right', which we will discuss in this book, you'll find capital growth and appreciation highly rewarding.

Let's take our second scenario: capital growth from buying at a price below the market value. In this example, let's say you purchased a property 20% below the market value. With this being the case, you'd have gained 20% in capital growth from day one. If the property was valued at £100,000 in its present condition, and you purchased the property at £80,000, this represents a 20% below market value discount, giving you an instant £20,000 upside. Don't worry, we'll discuss how you can achieve discounts at this level and beyond.

Let's now discuss our third scenario: capital growth by adding value through renovating the property. Let's say you purchased a property valued at £100,000, which required a full renovation. After the renovation, providing the numbers work, which we'll discuss later in this book, you find yourself with a property revalued at £150,000, allowing you to benefit from rapid capital growth.

Not everyone will wish to buy and hold property, and capital growth doesn't necessarily have to come from holding, which you can start to see here, and which will become clearer as we move through the book. Some people will choose to buy-to-flip, or trade deals, which we'll discuss when we come to investment strategies. The important thing to keep in mind, is that if you choose not to have buy-to-let as your primary strategy, you still have the option to cherry pick the best deals for your own portfolio, as and when they come about.

RENTAL INCOME

While holding buy-to-let properties for the long-term, providing you find deals that meet predetermined and strict investment criteria, and you buy right, you can benefit from monthly cashflow in the form of rental income.

The idea with rental income, is that the rent paid by your tenant will cover your expenses, such as mortgage payments, insurance, and other associated costs. After expenses have been paid, what remains is your profit. I'd suggest that as a rule of thumb, the lowest amount in terms of profit that you should be willing to accept is £250 per month per property under £100,000. You can then double that amount for every £100,000 on top. So if a property is £200,000, you'd be looking for a minimum of £500 per month profit after all expenses.

At Property Protege ™ we like to have people determine their financial freedom figure; the magic number that they would need coming in month after month to cover all expenses. This is not about becoming a millionaire or the next host of the The Apprentice. It's about determining the lowest amount you would need coming in, to allow you the freedom to live life on your own terms, and giving you the platform to build an even stronger property business.

Let's say your financial freedom figure was £2,500, and you earned a modest £250 profit per property per month after all expenses, on ten buy-to-let properties…

Job done. You have enough coming in, to allow you the freedom that many can only dream of.

Now, it's important to mention that when building a buy-to-let portfolio, we shouldn't be spending all of our profit. We have to budget for contingencies, void periods, repairs, tax, and so on. But let's not get ahead of ourselves. We'll show you in the coming chapters how to buy and build your portfolio properly, for maximum benefit and reward.

If you don't like the idea of holding property and having tenants, you may consider property development in the form of 'flips', or property deal trading, as strategies to replace your income and create financial freedom much faster.

CASHFLOW

Let's continue with the example of £2,500 per month as a financial freedom figure, which equates to £30,000 per annum, but let's say you chose not to focus on buy-to-let. Let's say you sourced a property, purchased it, added value by renovating it, and put it back on the market, banking the same £30,000 in one flip. Or, you could do three smaller flips with £10,000 profit per deal inside one year, or if you want to aggressively pursue this, you could do many more. The buy-to-flip strategy is great for cashflow as, when done right, you should be turning each flip around inside six months, releasing the profit and creating strong cashflow.

For those of you wondering how on earth you're going to buy ten properties, or buy and renovate to flip, then you fall into the same category I was in upon starting, which is having zero deposit funds or cash for renovations. Don't worry; we have you covered. My suggestion would be to start as I did, with property trading. I'll explain more on this when we reach our investment strategies section of the book. For now, just know that the average our Property Protege ™ students are achieving, is no less than £7,500 per deal by trading property. That means, in this example, you would only need to trade four properties per annum, which is one every three months to hit your freedom figure. Not too difficult, right? Well, this is the very least I'd hope you would achieve. This is property we're talking about here. The sky is the limit, as they say.

When I started in property, I wasn't in a position to buy. I had no credit, and no funds to invest.

Deal trading, or packaging deals, was my way in. It was pure cashflow. Bread and butter.

Just as I started in property by trading deals for cashflow, we still focus heavily on this strategy with our Property Proteges to this day. Whilst many other strategies have come and gone, property deal trading has stood the test of time and has been a consistent winner in allowing rapid income.

If you're looking for a way in, and don't have the funds to buy at this point in time, this is it.

If you're looking for a way to replace your income fast, this is it.

BUSINESS

Whatever your primary strategy in property is, many people reading this will choose to make it their full-time business. There are an unlimited number of routes you could take to make property your full-time focus, and an unlimited number of ways you can earn additional income.

Building a property business means that as well as focusing on your primary strategies and business model, you begin to play the game at a higher level by focusing on multiple streams of property income.

One of the core strategies in building a property business, can involve the buy-to-flip strategy, where you buy a property that needs work, and you project manage, or bring in a project manager, to oversee the renovation, before selling the property on the open market. Projects such as this can be highly lucrative, and involve a keen eye for the numbers, the ability to source or access deals, and the ability to raise finance from third parties to ensure you aren't limited in the number of projects you can work on.

It's all good fun, it's exciting, and it's highly lucrative.

It's also not that difficult when you understand the moving parts.

We'll discuss buy-to-flip and other income streams in more detail as we progress.

LIFESTYLE

Property, as we've discussed, can make you very wealthy. You can play the long-term game, whilst enjoying rental income. You can very quickly produce strong cashflow through trading / packaging deals. You can build a business through buy-to-flip strategies or building a portfolio, as well as benefitting from multiple other income streams.

But why do we do any of this?

Of course, business is exciting, but there has to be other reasons. Being in property can afford you the life and the lifestyle you desire. If you've ever longed for the opportunity to afford your dream car, or dream house, or security for your family, or better schooling, or exciting holidays; whatever drives you, and for whatever reason you find yourself reading this book, it's all possible when you follow the system and do the work.

This is property.

If you get this right, you can make serious changes in your life…

You could move on to purchase your dream home, you could end up purchasing your dream cars, you could create wealth to contribute more to your church, you could raise funds for worthy causes, you could travel the world, you could create security and freedom for your family, you could give your children what you may not have had growing up, you could support others on their own journey. The choices are unlimited. It's your life. You have one shot. What do you want to do with it? Through property, you could literally give yourself the keys.

THE FOUNDATIONS

Now that we know why property is our number one investment vehicle, let's look at the foundations.

The property foundations are just as important as the mindset. When you understand the foundations, everything else will fall into place. I'll give you the overview here, and we'll dig deeper as we go through the book.

DO YOU NEED MONEY TO INVEST, TO GET STARTED?

Often, I'm asked if it's possible to start in property with no money.

Here's the reality…

Whilst being the single most common objection for new people getting started, starting in property with no money can actually be an advantage.

Naturally, I get funny looks with this statement, so please allow me to explain.

Let's say you were in the position of having £150,000 to invest. Sure, we can, and will, show you how to put it to work throughout this book for the best possible return, but once that money is out to work, you'd be in the exact same position as someone with no initial start-up capital.

With this in mind, learning how to raise finance, which we'll cover later in the book, is a vital skill that you must master in order to enjoy lasting success in property. It's never a question of resources. It's always a question of resourcefulness.

But let's say you do in fact have money to invest. Awesome. You can put it to work very quickly, and watch it grow through continual reinvestment over time. That being said, I would always suggest that your focus should be on raising funds through commercial funding, private funding, and also unconventional methods. If this is new language to you, or you can hear the little voice in your head telling you that this is all too complicated for you, then relax, because we're going to break this down and show you just how possible it is.

KNOWING AND COMMITTING TO YOUR STRATEGY

Later in the book, we'll look at the various strategies available, but at this point it's important to highlight that as a property professional, you must decide upon, commit to, and aggressively pursue a chosen strategy.

A short-term cashflow strategy, if you're starting with no money and have a level of desperation in making ends meet, could be trading deals, where you source below market value, discounted properties, or properties where you can add substantial value, package them up with a pretty bow on top, and sell the deal. This is how I started in property and it is how I made my first seven-figure sum; by committing to, and dominating, in this one specific strategy. For the same reason, this is what we teach our Property Protege ™ students as a means to creating cashflow and freeing themselves from full-time employment in as fast a time as possible.

A short to mid-term strategy could be buying to flip, where you'd buy a discounted property, or certainly one where you know you can add value, then renovate and sell.

A longer-term strategy could be buying to hold, where you'd buy below market value, perform a light renovation, and rent the property to tenants, enjoying the monthly rental income (taking a real look at what you should spend and what you should save for contingencies), and benefiting from capital growth over the long-term.

Being focused on a chosen strategy is vitally important.

My recommendation to new investors, is to treat your property business as a business, not a hobby, and to do what any other business would, by having a short-term cashflow strategy, as well as a longer-term focus. You need cashflow to survive. You also need the big picture, to thrive.

THE WHERE AND THE WHAT

When you know where you're starting from, and you've c(¬¬itted to your chosen strategies, you're going to have to start thinking a¹ going to invest or trade. We call this location your G(again, this is content we'll be covering throughout the should be on mastering your Goldmine Area, in order the local market in every way possible.

Once you know where you'll be investing or trading, the next thing you'd want to do is identify the types of property you'd be looking at. There are many property types you'll come across, including cottage flats, tenement flats, bungalows, semi-detached, detached, mid-terraced, and so on. The strategy you choose to follow, will largely determine the property type you'll focus on.

And then we go a level deeper again. Will you be looking at properties with 1 bedroom, 2 bedrooms, 3 bedrooms? Will you be looking for students, working professionals, or families? You're only going to know this, when you determine your Goldmine Area, and you're only going to determine your Goldmine Area, when you know the strategy you'll choose to focus on; all of which we're going to explore.

FINDING THE DEALS

Once you've decided upon a strategy, your Goldmine Area, the property type you'll go for, and you understand the numbers that are possible with your deals, you're going to have to start finding those deals.

What is a deal?

A deal is when you can acquire a property (or secure your interests in a property in order to sell the deal without ever having to buy the property) at a price below the market value. So if a property is valued at £100,000, you'd be looking to gain a substantial discount. That being said, the discount isn't always the most important aspect. What matters, is knowing what the property will be worth when you add value, providing your focus is to flip the property. If your focus is holding for the long-term, the discount will be important to you. If your focus is trading the deal, then you'd want to know all of the moving parts in order to have your deal be seen as an attractive prospect to potential investors, be their strategy to hold, or flip.

So where do you find the deals?

That's where strategic marketing comes into play. We'll cover this in detail later.

Many amateur investors focus on RightMove, on building relationships with estate agents and certain types of investors, in the hope of being passed the Holy Grail. Sure, there's merit to each of these strategies, but it's a slow, long, arduous, and tiresome game, and no sourcer or agent is going to bring you enough deals to build a business. This is why you must make marketing and deal sourcing your own responsibility and not rely on the efforts of others. Once you've gone through the marketing section of this book, all of this will make perfect sense.

More experienced and professional investors are carrying out direct-to-vendor marketing campaigns.

Let me be clear here. Your role in property, should also benefit sellers. You're not taking advantage of anyone's situation; you're helping people out of the situation they've found themselves in.

This includes people who are separating, people who are emigrating and their house sale has fallen through, people who are facing repossession, people who are in financial difficulty, people who are downsizing, people who have inherited a property, and people who find themselves in a broken chain. All sorts of people from all walks of life. They're your friends, your family, your neighbours, the people down at the local pub, the people you pass in the street. Your focus, is on becoming that local property specialist, and being the only sensible option when it comes to property related solutions.

MASTERING THE FIGURES

The final foundational element to consider, before we discuss the property purchase process, is the figures. We must master the figures.

Too many amateur investors make costly mistakes because they fail to conduct the appropriate due diligence. They get excited and think that what they're doing is a good deal, but if you don't do the right checks, the appropriate due diligence, then you can't be sure you're actually buying or involving yourself in an investment that's going to make money. Simple oversights lead to disaster. It's vital to get this right.

With all of this in mind, let's shift through the gears, and focus on the property purchase process.

We know we must determine our strategy. We know we must determine our Goldmine Area. We know we must determine our target market and the specific properties we'll take into consideration in our target area. We know we must carry out aggressive marketing in order to find the deals. We know we must master the figures, to avoid disaster, and to enjoy some serious upside.

But let's slow down, and get into the bare bones of it.
Let's talk about the property purchase process.

THE PROPERTY PURCHASE PROCESS

If you haven't yet purchased a property, your own or for investment purposes, this is going to be highly relevant and important. On the other hand, even if you have purchased a property, I encourage you to read and fully understand what follows, as it forms the system that you'll be following when you buy-to-let, buy-to-flip, or source to then sell onto other investors. It's important.

When I first started, I was excited, but plagued with doubt. I was hyper and fearful, simultaneously. I was 20 when I bought my first property. I was feeling the pressure. I was feeling rushed by the estate agent. My mortgage broker was asking questions that I didn't understand and didn't know the answer to. Everything was new to me. I had no one to walk me through it. I wanted to take advice, but I was afraid that the people I was dealing with would sense my naivety and take advantage. I was about to take out a loan that was triple the amount of my annual salary. It was pretty terrifying.

Nowadays, looking back, I have a little chuckle.

What was once a nightmare, is now a daily activity.

It's the new normal we discussed in our mindset section. It's the comfort zone stretch that we all go through when stepping into a new realm, before realising it's actually pretty simple, and not all that complicated. Once you're at the point of having purchased multiple properties, there will come a time when you're just signing paperwork with no worries, because you've conducted thorough due diligence, you know your numbers, and it's an unemotional process. However, the first one can be scary, so let's take time to understand the process.

FIND A GOOD MORTGAGE BROKER

The first step in the property purchase process is to find a good mortgage broker. Notice I said the word 'good', I didn't say, "find a mortgage broker".

You wouldn't want to walk into the bank, inexperienced and uneasy, and take their in-house broker. You'd want to find a broker who has access to the whole of market; someone who has your best interests at heart and who is not simply there to push for the mortgage product or lender that lends them the most commission. You'll want a broker who will find a mortgage that is suitable for you and your circumstances. More importantly, someone who will communicate with you and walk you comfortably through the entire process.

When you find your ideal mortgage broker, you're going to ask them to carry out a DIP (Decision In Principle). They'll then ask you to fill out a key-facts illustration, which is just information about yourself. You will give this to the mortgage broker who will then go to the marketplace and identify which mortgage lenders would be right for you, based on your own circumstances. They'll look at multiple factors, including finances, income, credit, and so on, to ascertain eligibility. At this point in the process, you'll know what you're eligible for, first and foremost, and how much you can obtain.

A little side-note: as you'll learn throughout this book, as an investor or trader, you don't necessarily have to be the person buying the property. Even if you're going to be a partner in a property, this can be through a company, or with a joint venture partner. If you plan on aggressively pursuing property as a business, you'll very quickly reach your cap in terms of being able to obtain a mortgage if solely focused on traditional buy-to-let mortgages. This is where a good mortgage broker will earn their worth, by forward planning and offering non-traditional lending, which we'll cover later in the book. The important thing to note in this section of the book is an understanding of the process.

VIEW THE PROPERTY

The second part of the property purchase process, or the first depending on how you look at it, is to go out and view property on the market or sourced through your own marketing efforts. That doesn't mean you need to look at properties with a maximum price of, let's say £100,000, if that was your mortgage eligibility. You can look at properties which are worth less, or even worth more, because when we chat about negotiation, you'll learn that you can negotiate these properties to well below the asking price.

What I would encourage you to do when identifying properties in your Goldmine Area, is to go out and view a number of properties on the market to get a general feel for the viewing process. You'll also meet some estate agents and viewing agents, which will allow you to begin building relationships. Sometimes, when viewing through traditional means, you'll even come into direct contact with the seller.

When viewing properties, it's important that we start to become comfortable with the process, and being able to know (it is your Goldmine Area after all) what work needs done (kitchens, bathrooms and so on) from the point of view of what it's likely to cost, and what it's likely to return on the other side.

I would suggest that you view some walk-in condition properties within your Goldmine Area, to have a look and get a feel for what standard of finish will be required when you're renovating properties to obtain higher values.

REQUEST THE HOME REPORT

If you're buying a property on the market in Scotland, you'll benefit from having access to what's known as a Home Report. In this document, which can be requested from the estate agent, you'll be able to see what the market value is, information on various aspects of the property, information on required repairs, and so on. If you're at that point, you may also want to look at getting a builder to look at the property with you to identify whether they can resolve any issues shown in the Home Report.

HAVE A VALUATION CARRIED OUT

If you're buying property throughout the rest of the UK outside Scotland, then at this stage you'd look for a valuation to be carried out. The surveyor would be able to identify any potential issues with the property. Remember however, that at this point in your own personal journey, you're simply trying to get familiar with the viewing process, identify any issues, take some photographs, and potentially have a video walkthrough so that you can start to feel comfortable with viewing properties, and more importantly, being aware of what you should look out for.

MAKE AN OFFER

Once you've reviewed the Home Report or had the valuation carried out, and after you've run the numbers, you'd make an offer on the property. To do this, you'd either make a verbal offer to the estate agent to find out if the seller is interested in accepting, after which, if the seller is happy to proceed, you would instruct your solicitor to make a formal offer. Alternatively, you may go directly to your solicitor and have them submit the formal offer to the estate agent or the seller's solicitor, allowing them to make a decision.

Your solicitor will be a core member of your power team who will walk you through the entire property purchase process, keeping you in the loop and communicating on how things are going. Your solicitor is going to do all of the legal searches required, including checks for any underlying issues, and more importantly, handle the conveyancing process which allows you to buy the property.

The examples given here, are to give you clarity on the purchase process, however, through your marketing, you'll be going direct to vendor, and using your new found negotiation skills to agree upon numbers that work for you as the investor, and for the seller. Your solicitor would then take it from there.

FIND A LETTING AGENT

At the point of having your offer accepted, you'd want to be proactive. You don't have to wait until the purchase process is complete to find a letting agent. You'd want the property tenanted as soon as possible, and as such, you'd work to ensure a good local agent was in place. To achieve this, you'd want to speak with several agents, to ensure you find someone who will work for you in multiple ways.

Your letting agent, upon understanding the timeframe for the interior renovation, will work with you to ensure the property is at a standard that will attract tenants and minimise potential void periods. They will then work to rent your property as soon as possible, and will carry out all relevant searches and checks on prospective tenants, as well as covering all bases from their perspective, and from yours.

FIND A BUILDER

At the same point as finding a letting agent in your first purchase, you'd also want to look for a builder. The ideal scenario here is that if any renovation work is required, you'd want your builder to view the property with you. You can request a separate viewing where you take your builder with you, where they can begin calculating what needs done, and give you a quotation if required. Another reason to have your builder view the property is so that when the purchase is complete, you can simply hand the keys to the builder on the day of completion and have them start work. This then ensures the renovation moves faster, again, minimising potential void periods.

PROCEEDING TO FULL MORTGAGE APPLICATION

Now that you've agreed upon the purchase price, you've liaised with your builder and letting agent, and your offer has been accepted, this is the point when your mortgage broker would submit the full mortgage application to the lender. Effectively, all this means is that your lender looks at the property you're purchasing, and providing all is well, which may include having their own surveyor ensure everything is as it should be, they will then approve the release of funds.

EXCHANGE / CONCLUDE MISSIVES

When funds are being released, you would exchange and complete, or 'conclude missives' as it were, on your property purchase. In Scotland, you'd conclude missives, which is effectively binding the contract, tying you into the deal and completing on the same day. You're going to get some people who will try to push you to conclude missives before you complete, perhaps a few weeks in advance. Don't be swayed or tempted to do this. You'd want to conclude missives and complete on the same day in Scotland, so keep that in mind.

If you're south of the Scottish border, in England and elsewhere in the UK, you would conclude contracts on the property transaction and then complete several weeks later. The reason you would conclude contracts prior to completing is to protect yourself from someone else coming in with a more attractive offer. You would however only conclude contracts once you are certain that everything checks out after the survey report and with your mortgage lender being happy to lend on the property.

PAY YOUR DEPOSIT

When you complete and conclude missives (or contracts) on your property purchase, you will then have to pay your deposit. If your lender is going to give you 75% of the loan (known as loan to value); then you would pay £25,000 on a £100,000 property, with the lender putting in £75,000. The £25,000 is your deposit. You would send the deposit to your solicitor, and then the mortgage lender would release the other 75%. Your solicitor would then have 100% of the funds required, which would be sent to the seller's solicitor.

Now, let's jump back a little...

Your conveyancing solicitor is going to ask you for three months bank statements, to see where the deposit funds are coming from. This is for money laundering and regulatory purposes. They will also ask for ID, and have you sign various contracts. If this is your first purchase it may seem daunting, but don't worry, this is all simply part of the buying process, and you will want your solicitor to talk and walk you through each step.

Providing everything checks out, your solicitor would then send the funds to the seller's solicitor, and complete the transaction, allowing you to take ownership of the property. Also, at this stage you will have the additional fees to pay such as your solicitor's conveyancing fee and potentially the mortgage broker will require their fee be paid (normally payable on successful mortgage application). As well as these fees you will have an additional amount of Land and Building Transaction Tax (LBTT) known as the Additional Dwelling Supplement (the ADS), due on the purchase of additional dwellings in Scotland for buy-to-let properties and second homes. In England and Ireland, this is called Stamp Duty Land Tax (SDLT). In Wales it's called Land Transaction Tax (LTT). Your Solicitor will inform you of the required amounts as this differs throughout the UK, and the percentage is calculated in different increments based on the value of the property.

A quick note on the additional tax that landlords are now faced with in 2018 (time of writing). My view is we simply have to factor in the additional costs in our due diligence, to ensure the numbers still work for our investment criteria. If we are buying right by identifying properties, negotiating well, and adding value, we have nothing to worry about when it comes to the various taxes.

RENOVATE, THEN LET, OR SELL

At this point, you now have complete ownership of the property. You'd now want to get your builders in, to start the required renovation. As the renovation comes to conclusion, providing you have a proactive letting agent, you'd hope to have a tenant ready to move in. If your strategy is not to hold the property as a buy-to-let, rather you are looking to sell the property on the open market as a buy-to-flip, then you'd have your estate agent lined up to market the property on the open market.

And that's it.

Let's not complicate it.

As you'll find out as we progress through *Your Property Jumpstart* ™, this isn't difficult.

Now let's take a moment to look at what happens after you buy.

WHAT HAPPENS AFTER YOU BUY?

So, you've purchased your first property. You've decided to let out the property (as opposed to flip the property on the open market or trade the deal without ever buying).

So, what happens next with your buy-to-let?

As you might imagine, there will be a number of costs involved. The last thing you'll want, are any surprises.

LETTING AGENTS

We've already had the chat about letting agents, but what we haven't discussed are their fees. Your letting agent is going to take an average of 10% of the monthly rent, each month. The letting agent is also going to have upfront marketing costs that must be factored in. This will generally come as your set-up and marketing fee, which is normally, but not always, half the monthly rent. The marketing fee simply covers the costs to market your property and find a tenant. The set-up fee is for the agent to conduct due diligence on the tenant, complete reference checks, arrange tenancy agreements, and cover their own time for doing so.

As a landlord, you will have a legal responsibility to have certain checks carried out and certain boxes ticked before tenanting a property. Your letting agent will guide you through this process and handle most of the heavy lifting, including letting you know when you'll have to refresh and update in each area. This is a good thing, as it covers and protects not only your tenant, but also you, as the landlord.

TENANCY INVENTORY REPORTS

Inventory reports are one of the most important documents related to your property. The inventory report will accurately describe the condition of the property, with photographs taken, which can then be used to assess claims for damages or substantial changes at the end of the tenancy. Inventory reports should be as detailed as possible, and are essential for resolving deposit disputes at the end of the tenancy. It's important to note that inventory checks are not a legal requirement, but I strongly recommend you ensure this is in place, and any good letting agent will have this as standard practice.

ENERGY PERFORMANCE CERTIFICATE (EPC)

As a landlord, you have a legal responsibility to have an energy performance certificate (EPC). EPCs tell you how energy efficient a building is, and gives it a rating from A (very efficient) to G (inefficient). EPCs let the person renting the property know how costly it will be to heat and run. EPCs are valid for 10 years. In Scotland, the certificate is included in the Home Report.

GAS SAFETY CERTIFICATE

As a landlord, you have a legal responsibility to have a gas safety certificate and report from a qualified gas safety engineer. This check must be carried out annually, on all gas appliances and installations. The engineer will provide you with the gas safety record, detailing each appliance tested, results of safety checks, issues identified during checks, and actions or work required.

ELECTRICAL SAFETY CERTIFICATE

As a landlord, you have a legal responsibility to ensure that the electrical installation in a rented property is safe when tenants move in and is maintained in a safe condition throughout the duration. It's important to ensure a qualified electrician ticks the relevant boxes when a tenancy begins, and in order to comply with regulatory obligations and have periodic inspections carried out every five years to cover your bases.

LEGIONELLA TESTING

Legionnaires' disease is a potentially fatal form of pneumonia caused by the inhalation of small droplets of contaminated water containing legionella. Health and safety law does not require you to produce or obtain a legionnaires testing certificate, but as a landlord, you have a legal responsibility to ensure the health and safety of your tenant by keeping the property safe and free from health hazards, and assessing such risks.

FIRE SAFETY

As a landlord, it's your responsibility to fit and test smoke alarms and carbon monoxide alarms, as well as follow fire safety regulations for your properties. As with your inventory reports, EPCs, legionella testing, and gas and electrical safety certs, your letting agent will assist you in this matter.

LANDLORD REGISTRATION (SCOTLAND)

If you're a landlord renting out a property in Scotland, you must register with Landlord Registration via their central system. That being said, if you own more properties in different parts of the country, you'll have to register as a landlord on the system for each area. Your registration will be valid for three years from the date that each local council approve the application.

This is your responsibility, although your Letting Agent may be ab assist you.

VOID PERIODS

This is something that many people don't take into account. If you're carrying out a renovation on a property, you're going to be the one responsible for paying the monthly mortgage payment throughout the weeks or months that it may take to carry out the renovation. You will also need to cover your gas and electric bills during voids. Voids also come into play in times where there is no tenant in the property after renovation, hence the need to buy right in the first place with thorough due diligence, and have a good letting agent in place.

COUNCIL TAX

Council tax is the responsibility of the tenant while the property is tenanted. However, if the property is unfurnished (during renovation or while vacant), you can apply for a council tax exemption. If your property is furnished, you as the landlord will be liable to pay council tax on the property at a discounted rate of up to 50 per cent. However, many local authorities apply a lower rate of discount in order to deter people from keeping properties empty. Once again, your letting agent will be able to assist, but be proactive, and do not assume they will initiate this on your behalf

LANDLORDS INSURANCE

There's no legal obligation for a landlord to take out a dedicated insurance policy. However, if you have a mortgage on your property it's very likely that your lender will require you to take out appropriate insurance before taking on tenants. There are various insurance products available, including buildings insurance, contents cover, loss of rent, and property owners Public Liability. Although landlord's insurance isn't a legal requirement (aside from any requirements and conditions set by your lender), it does provide useful cover to protect your investment. Let's be real. Things can go wrong. The worst time to need landlord's insurance, is when it's too late.

nsurance covers the big issues, you're also going to have to the little things. You're going to want tenants who'll be residing in the property for a number of years and who will look after it as their own, however, you never know when a window will shatter, or a boiler will break, or pipes will freeze, or any number of issues that, I can assure you, will happen. My recommendation, is that you keep at least 10% of the monthly rent aside for contingencies and unforeseen repairs and maintenance.

Ok, so, still want to be a landlord?

Awesome.

Don't let the number of boxes needing ticked scare you.

Instead, understand them. Factor them in. Include them in the numbers when you first assess the property at the due diligence stage.

We'll come back to this later when running some examples.

I realise this section of *Your Property Jumpstart* ™ has been quite heavy. I'd love to say it's going to get lighter, but it's not. Let's break down the property jargon that's thrown around, so that you truly begin to understand the game. Again, don't let this scare you. It's better to be armed, and this book, *Your Property Jumpstart* ™, is your road map to financial success in property.

PROPERTY JARGON

Just recently, I was reading Tony Robbins' latest book: Money. Early in the book, Tony references the medical world and tells us that 225,000 people have died of "Iatrogenic deaths" in the past year. According to the American Medical Association, it's the third largest cause of death in the United States.

So what does it mean? It sounds important. Is it a rare tropical disease? A genetic mutation?

No. Iatrogenic refers to an accidental death caused by a doctor, or a hospital, or an incorrect or unnecessary procedure.

So why don't they just say so? Simply, because it doesn't serve a medical institutions interests to put it in plain language a layperson can understand.

The property world has its own jargon too...

Agricultural covenant, APR, AST, Base Rate, BMV, Break Clause, Broker, BTL, Capital Rest, Broken Chains, Compulsory Purchase Orders, Conveyancing, DIP, Disbursements, Discounted Tracker Rate, ERP, ERC, Endowment, EPC, Equitable Interest, Equity, Freehold, Gazumping, Gearing, Gifted Deposit, HMO, HIP, HR, IFA, ISA, Lien, LTV, Loan-To-Value, Mortgage Indemnity Premium, OMV, Option Agreements, PCM, Peppercorn Rent, PEP, Probate, Redemption, ROI, ROTI, TRB, SARB, Self Certification, SVR, Title Deeds, Gross Yield, Net Yield...

There are many special words, phrases and abbreviations for things that are really just disguised in language that would make it impossible for you to realise that what you're doing is costing you more money, or that it exists simply as language familiar to those who are time-served in property, or operating in an official capacity.

Most similar systems are designed to be confusing, so you'll give up control to the professionals who reap enormous fees by keeping you in the dark.

Allow me to be your translator.

Allow me to help you from feeling like you're in over your head.

The truth is, people in property don't generally walk around using fancy language, but the following guide will be your backup for when it's required.

For now, let's cover basic investment terms.

MORTGAGES

When you're about to apply for a mortgage, you're going to hear about the difference between 'interest only mortgages' and 'repayment mortgages'. Let's look at this in more detail.

When obtaining a mortgage for your own personal home, and paying the mortgage over time, this is not an asset, nor is it an investment. It costs you money, which means its an expense. Sure, it will rise in value over time and you may choose to release equity, but if you're servicing the building, then it is not an income producing asset or investment.

In most cases, with your own home, you'd obtain a repayment mortgage so that each monthly payment goes towards both the interest and the mortgage. For example, if you had a 25 year term, then come the end of the 25 years, you'd have paid off 100% of the interest and 100% of the loan, meaning you'd be left with no mortgage on your personal property.

On the flip side, when you have an investment property, you wouldn't be looking to pay down the mortgage. You would instead maximise the rental income by paying interest only, meaning much lower monthly payments and much more left over.

Using the 25 years example previously discussed on your own home, with an investment property, you'd reach the end of the 25 years, and you wouldn't have paid anything other than the interest. So how is that a benefit or advantage?

Think back to our earlier discussion about capital growth; the increase in a property's value over time. Here's one thing you can be sure of…

The value of the property will increase, and at the end of the 25 years, upon selling or refinancing, you're going to be able to pay off the mortgage.

"But what if the property doesn't increase in value in 25 years?"

Crazy question, right? But one that some will ask.

In the investment strategy section, we're going to talk about how to make money when you buy. The first thing to note, is that you're never going to be paying full market value for your property. You should always buy at a discount. So let's say you bought at 20% discount, and property prices didn't budge an inch in 25 years, whilst you cover nothing more than the interest. No problem, because you'll still have 20% equity. So in 25 years time, when you go to sell the property, you'll have 20% equity which means you can pay off your mortgage and still profit.

You may be wondering why we haven't included your deposit in the equity above, as surely those funds should count for something? Be patient young Jedi, we'll be showing you very soon how to pull your deposit funds out not too long after having purchased the property.

So to recap: when buying your own home, you'll want a capital repayment mortgage. If someone else is going to service that debt by renting the property from you, then you'd want an interest only mortgage, to maximise rental income.

MORTGAGE PRODUCT TERMS

In the world of mortgages, you're going to hear terms such as tracker, fixed rate, variable, offset, and more. Once again, don't be frightened off by this. Your broker and power team members are here to help with each moving part of the property purchase process.

To simplify and give you an example, let's look at the following...

Let's say you had a tracker mortgage. All this means is that it tracks the Bank of England base rate. If the Bank of England's base rate increases by 1%, then your mortgage rate goes up by 1%. For example, if you have 4% on your tracker mortgage and the Bank of England goes up by 1%, then your mortgage interest rate increases to 5% in this example.

Let's say you're on a fixed rate, getting a fixed percentage for a set period of time. All this means, is if the Bank of England base rate increases or decreases, nothing would change for you. This means you have peace of mind knowing that over the next five years, for example, you're going to have a fixed rate interest percentage and it does not matter whether the base rate goes up or down. You will only be paying interest on the fixed rate agreed upon.

EARLY REDEMPTION CHARGES OR PENALTIES

Something else you'd want to be aware of when it comes to mortgage terms, is early redemption penalties and charges. Let's say your exit strategy was a buy-to-flip. You'd want to make sure that you'd be with a mortgage lender that didn't have high penalties for redeeming on your mortgage early, which you would be, by buying only for a short time. With this in mind, it's important to be clear with your broker on your proposed exit strategy so they can find the right mortgage for you.

LENDERS VALUATION FEE

Lenders are going to have their own valuation fee. Whether you've carried out your own independent valuation or not, and whether a Home Report is in place or not, the lender will want to carry out their own valuation. They will then pass the charge on to you, which will normally be a few hundred pounds. Again, your Mortgage broker will advise you on how much that will be, as it's going to be different for different lenders. The lender carrying out their own valuation simply means they'll send out their own Surveyor to look at the property, to make sure it's worth what you're about to pay for it, and to make sure there are no underlying issues.

ARRANGEMENT FEE

An arrangement fee is charged for arranging the finance on the mortgage. The good thing about arrangement fees, is that you can add them to the mortgage loan amount. This means you don't have to pay them upfront although you can if you choose to. The majority of investors add this to the mortgage, as it can be a few thousand pounds, or a percentage of the mortgage. Sure, you'll pay a little interest on it, but you'll save upfront. Again, your mortgage lender will advise you on what the fee will be.

COMMERCIAL FUNDING

When you speak with your Mortgage broker they'll let you know about personal lending through traditional high street lenders. This is standard. However, they may also make you aware of commercial funding. Commercial funding can allow you to buy and own properties as a limited company, even if that company is new. The commercial route is also a great way to get lending on properties that are deemed un-mortgageable by traditional high street lenders due to the extensive level of renovation work required.

Commercial lending or bridging tends to be more expensive than traditional lending, but you really have to look at your own situation and eligibility. Don't get too caught up in the extra percentages and fees if this is your only option. If there is still money to be made in a deal once you've factored in the extra costs, then do the deal.

YIELD (INCOME RETURN ON INVESTMENT)

There are two types of yield: Gross Yield and Net Yield. Let's explore.

GROSS YIELD

Gross Yield, is simply your Annual Rent (AR), divided by your property's Purchase Price (PP), multiplied by 100, to give you the percentage:

$$(AR \div PP) \times 100$$

For example, if your Annual Rent is £6,000 and your Purchase Price was £75,000, you would divide £6,000 by £75,000, giving 0.08. That multiplied by 100, gives us **8% Gross Yield**.

A yield above 7% is a good deal.

Naturally, the higher the Gross Yield, particularly when over 10%, the better the deal.

NET YIELD

Net Yield is where you would take associated expenses into account. So if we use our previous example, where the Annual Rent (AR) was £6,000, we would then deduct our Annual Expenses (AE), dividing that resulting figure by the property Purchase Price (PP), and finally multiplying by 100 to give us the Net Yield percentage

$$((AR - AE) \div PP) \times 100$$

Let's take a moment to talk about monthly expenses.

The first of your monthly expenses is the mortgage payment. In this example, with your interest only mortgage, let's say it's £150.

The next of your monthly expenses is your letting agent fees. You are NOT going to manage your own properties. You're going to outsource to a letting agent, as with all other professional services. Your time should be spent sourcing deals and raising finance, whilst leveraging experts in their relative fields to do what they do best. In this case, with £500 per month rent, your 10% letting agent fee would be £50.

Next on your monthly expenses might be your buildings insurance and factors fees. If you have a factor in place this would go towards communal repairs to the building, ongoing maintenance and so on. Let's say the building insurance and factor fees are £25 per month.

You may also want to account for additional insurances such as boiler cover and landlord's insurance. Let's say that's another £25.

So in this case, you have…

- Mortgage Payments: £150
- Letting Agency Fees: £50
- Building Insurance and Factor Fees: £25
- Additional Insurances: £25

Annual Expenses = £3,000 (12 months of £250 expenses)

£6,000 Annual Rent less £3,000 Annual Expenses leaves you with £3,000.

If we divide our £3,000 by the property Purchase Price of £75,000, giving us 0.04, x 100, we have a 4% Net Yield. So as you can see, the net is quite simply taking expenses into account.

There are other expenses which I haven't covered, which we will go over in greater detail within the due diligence section, but these are the typical primary expenses which should be used when calculating your Net Yield.

You might be wondering, why do I need to know all of this?

All will be revealed.

When you can run the numbers and conduct thorough due diligence; essentially when you know a deal is a deal, you'll do very well in property.

BMV (BELOW MARKET VALUE)

BMV is a term you're going to hear repeatedly from many other property investors. BMV stands for 'below market value', and relates to the discount on a property. Essentially, the price you've negotiated below the market value price.

The calculation for this is as follows…

$$((PV - PP) \div PV) \times 100$$

So if the Property Value is £100,000, but you've negotiated a Purchase Price of £75,000, you'd calculate the BMV as follows…

- £100,000 - £75,000 = £25,000
- £25,000 ÷ £100,000 = 0.25
- 0.25 x 100 = **25% BMV**

So your deal, would be a 25% below market value deal.

As you work through *Your Property Jumpstart* ™, and we get into the core material including investment strategies, you're going to be looking to buy a property at a substantial discount. In fact, when you start your own marketing and begin to negotiate with sellers, you'll find yourself, more often than not, turning away from anything less than 25% below market value. That being said, it's not always about the discount, it's about the level to which we can increase the value. Acquiring a property at a substantial discount whilst also being able to substantially increase the value is a massive win. The big focus is on the end result.

RETURN ON CAPITAL EMPLOYED (FOR BUY-TO-LET)

ROCE (Return On Capital Employed) is where we find out the *real* return on the TMI (Total Money Invested) into a deal. When you're packaging deals for other investors, or looking for joint venture partners, this is what you'll want to show them, to demonstrate why they should invest in property; showing them the return they can achieve from property versus leaving their money in the bank.

Let's continue with the figures we've been using.

The calculation for this is as follows…

$$((AR - AE) \div TMI) \times 100$$

So using our numbers as above…

Our Annual Rent is £6,000. Our Annual Expenses are £3,000.

The property value is £100,000. We're buying at £75,000. We'd then be putting in a 25% deposit (of the purchase price, not the market value) of £18,750.

Let's say your legal fees, light renovation, and everything else rounds up to £5,000. This means you would have a total cash investment including deposit, legals, renovation, and any other associated costs of £23,750.

So let's do this…

- £6,000 - £3,000 = £3,000
- £3,000 ÷ £23,750 = 0.12
- 0.12 x 100 = **12.6% ROCE**

I want you to think about this for a moment: if you have £20,000 sitting in the bank, what return would you be getting?

RETURN ON CAPITAL EMPLOYED (FOR BUY-TO-FLIP)

Let's do the same calculation but this time we'll be looking at the return on investment as a buy-to-flip.

Let's continue with the figures we've been using, and incorporate the SP (Sale Price) and all expenses incurred.

The calculation for this is as follows...

$$((SP - expenses) \div TMI) \times 100$$

So using our numbers as above...

The property value is £100,000. We're buying at £75,000. We'd then be putting in a 25% deposit (of the purchase price, not the market value) of £18,750.

Let's say your legal fees, light renovation, and everything else rounds up to £5,000. This means you would have a total cash investment including deposit, legals, renovation, and any other associated costs of £23,750.

However, we must factor in some additional expenses. We need to factor in an additional set of legal fees for selling the property, estate agents costs to market the property, and a Home Report in Scotland (or potentially you'll have had a valuation report carried out).

When paying off the balance of the mortgage, and if you have added the arrangement fee to the mortgage, you will have to pay the outstanding mortgage and arrangement fee (and any redemption fee for redeeming early on your mortgage if there is one).

You should also factor in 6 months interest only mortgage payments that you will have been paying whilst the property remained unoccupied.

All expenses would be as follows...

- Deposit (25% of purchase price): £18,750
- Legal fees (for buying): £750
- Stamp duty (3% of purchase price): £2,250
- Light renovation: £2,000
- Legal fees (for selling): £750
- Estate agent fees: £1,000
- Home Report (or valuation): £500 HR
- Mortgage payments (6 months empty period): £1,200
- Outstanding mortgage (incl 3% arrangement fee): £57,937.50

Total Expenses = £85,137.50

Let's say you don't add any additional value and the property still has an end-value of £100,000 and it now sells at that price. Our calculation again:

$$((SP - Expenses) \div TMI) \times 100$$

- £100,000 - £85,137.50 = £14,862.50
- £14,862.50 $\div$ £23,750 = 0.625
- 0.625 x 100 = **62.5% ROCE**

I want you to think about this for a moment: if you have £20,000 sitting in the bank, what return would you be getting?

What we've just gone through in these examples, show that if you invest in property you could be getting a 12.6% return! Or as a buy-to-flip you would be making a 62.5% return!

This is why this calculation is vitally important, not just for your own investments, but to show investors or joint venture partners who could potentially invest with you. When I say investors, this can refer to property investors, high net-worth individuals, family members with savings, friends with funds that can be released from pension pots, and so on. But we're getting ahead of ourselves. It can also refer to those who may buy your packaged deals (property trading).

Think about it: as a flip in this example we see a 62.5% return on capital used. Don't you think that someone would want to partner with you and front *all* of the capital required for say a 50% profit share? Meaning that they would be getting a 31.25% return on their capital used. The fact you never had to put any money into the deal gives you an infinite return on your own investment. The only investment you made is your time and possibly a small amount in marketing costs to source the deal.

If you've ever wondered how you'd find someone to invest in your deals, or buy the deals from you, just think for a moment about these numbers, and realise that you won't have any shortage of hungry buyers ready to invest.

The best part is, that in the investment strategies section of *Your Property Jumpstart* ™, we will show you that after six months, when you refinance and pull all of the money out of the deal, you, or your investors are going to have an infinite return on the money invested, which means the initial investment funds come out of the deal, and you're making positive cashflow with no capital employed.

Getting excited yet?

You should be.

We've covered a lot of ground so far, and it's been heavy going. Hopefully this high note starts to put the game into perspective. Now, let's move into the fundamentals, and the key players you're going to want onside to bring your property business to life.

BONUS CONTENT

Visit YourPropertyJumpstart.com/bonus
for your secret bonus chapter, the Protege Deal Calculator,
and additional content and resources to support you
on your property journey

CHAPTER 3:
THE FUNDAMENTALS
AND YOUR PROPERTY POWER TEAM

So far, we've covered your property millionaire mindset.

We've discussed why property is your number one vehicle for financial success.

We've discussed the property purchase process.

We've discussed what happens after you buy.

We've pulled apart the most important terms in property jargon.

And we've dropped some little bombs throughout each section.

Now let's discuss the rules of the game.

Like any game, there are rules and guiding principles.

In this chapter, I'm going to share my 8 Key Fundamentals to success in property, followed by a breakdown of the various professionals you'll want in your corner.

After more than a decade in property, playing the game on an aggressive level, the 8 Key Fundamentals that follow are your principles for success. Ignore them at your peril.

FUNDAMENTAL 1:
ALWAYS DO YOUR DUE DILIGENCE

One of the most basic yet under-appreciated elements in property, is research. Do your due diligence. There are far too many investors caught up in the hype of investing, and the big numbers they think they'll make, that they forget to cross-check the figures. They don't have set investment criteria in place, and they don't do due diligence on the property itself.

As this is such an important element, we'll be covering this in the next chapter in detail, as it's vital that you get it right. You must know what you're looking for, you must ensure there are no hidden surprises or underlying issues, and most importantly, you must master the figures.

Let's not be amateurs about this. Be the professional.

Always do your homework.

FUNDAMENTAL 2:
MAKE YOUR OWN RULES AND STICK TO THEM

You must make your own rules, and stick to them. What does this mean?

Essentially, this refers to your investment criteria.

Your investment criteria, is your own set of standards for what constitutes a deal for *you*. It's your own rules and principles around what you're willing to invest in, flip, or trade.

You'll have rules for what constitutes a buy-to-let for your own portfolio.

You'll have rules for what constitutes a buy-to-flip.

You'll have an idea of what investors are looking for, particularly if you're smart about sourcing specific deals for them, and you'll have rules for what constitutes a buy-to-let or a buy-to-flip for them, in order to trade your deals on if they don't fit your *own* standards.

So why must we set and stick to rules?

Let's say you have a rule that for your own portfolio: 'a buy-to-let property must have positive cashflow of £250 per month'.

Then someone offers you a deal at £220, and you take it. When something else then comes up at £190, you're more likely to take that one too, because you've already broken your own rules and you'll break them again.

Amateur investors break their own rules, which is a huge mistake. If you follow this pattern, you're going to reduce your positive cashflow, which means when issues arise, you won't have the cashflow to deal with them. So, make your own rules, and stick to them.

At this point, you may be wondering what those rules should be. We'll get to that.

FUNDAMENTAL 3:
ALWAYS BUY AT A DISCOUNT (BMV)

Earlier, we discussed the importance of BMV discounts, or BMV deals. As we discussed, BMV is a term you're going to hear repeatedly from many other property investors. BMV stands for 'below market value', and relates to the discount on a property. Essentially, the price you've negotiated below the market value price.

And our third fundamental, is that you must always buy at a discount.

Here's a little teaser for you in advance of our investment strategies section…

You make money when you buy.

How is this possible?

By buying property at a discount.

When you buy property, you must go in with the mindset that the property will never rise in value, even though you know it will. If you go in with the idea that it'll never rise, but you've bought the property at a discount, then you've already made your money. You make money when you buy. Again, this will become clearer as we progress.

FUNDAMENTAL 4:
ALWAYS BUY IN AN AREA WITH HIGH RENTAL DEMAND

Let's imagine you had a deal with a 40% below market value discount.

On the face of it, this is a huge deal.

You could add the deal to your own portfolio, you could add value and flip, or you could trade the opportunity. Who wouldn't want to take it off your hands?

However, if the property is in an area that doesn't have a high rental demand, then it's going to take a long time to rent the property to a tenant. This then eats into your cashflow; and the money you thought you were going to make, just isn't there, and you end up haemorrhaging cash.

Providing you do your due diligence, and you know your Goldmine Area inside out, you'll know which locations have high rental demand. I'd recommend you speak with your letting agent, to understand the best spots in your target area for high rental demand.

If you wanted to take it a step further, you might want to put an ad on Gumtree, advertising a 3-bed cottage flat in your prospective location, and then wait to see how many people get in touch. If you have a large number of people who reach out, it gives a good indication that it's a high rental demand area. Another indication, is when a To Let board goes up, or an ad is put online, and the property is rented out within 48 hours.

As you select your Goldmine Area, and begin to study the area and truly master it, you'll start to see patterns emerge, and you'll get a great grasp of what's what.

FUNDAMENTAL 5:
BUY FOR CASHFLOW

If you're buying to let, or sourcing a property to sell to another investor, then you'll want to buy (or source) for cashflow. I'd recommend a minimum of £250 positive cashflow every month per property, after paying off expenses and associated costs.

If you know your financial freedom figure, and you buy for cashflow, you'll be able to work towards your overall cashflow figure, enabling you to go full-time, replace your income, or begin to build the dream life you had in mind.

Having strong cashflow also acts as a buffer for unexpected surprises.

FUNDAMENTAL 6:
HAVE AN ELEMENT OF TRADING IN YOUR BUSINESS

Several times, we've referenced trading, or sourcing.

But what does it mean?

As you'll understand by now, buying to let, means buying a property to let it to tenants. Naturally, as we now know, we'd be buying for cashflow, in an area with high rental demand, at a discount, after doing our due diligence, and based on our own rules or criteria.

Awesome, so we understand that part.

Buy-to-flip is buying a property at a discount, after doing our due diligence, based on our own rules and investment criteria for a flip, and then selling the property in a short span of time, generally after increasing the value, above and beyond the value already generated by buying BMV.

Great, so hopefully that part is making sense now too.

So what exactly is trading?

Buy-to-flips can come under the trading umbrella, but generally, when we refer to trading, we're referring to the process of packaging deals. All this means is that you would find the deals, do the due diligence, run the numbers, and present the opportunity to your preferred investors as both a buy-to-let or a buy-to-flip. You would pull together the various elements of the deal, put a pretty bow on top, and sell the deal on, without ever having to buy.

The great thing about trading, is that it can provide quick cashflow.

While you're working on your portfolio (the long-term game), or buying to flip (short/mid-term), having an element of trading, by sourcing and selling deals, can put money in your pocket fast, freeing you up to focus full-time on your property business. This is the strategy I put into play when I started on my own property journey, and it's a strategy we teach to our Property Protege ™ students, to enable them to build a stream of cashflow quickly, to give them choices while they work on their bigger game. That being said, the trades our students are doing are generally in the region of £7,000 to £9,000 for sourcing a deal, running the numbers, securing the deal, and then selling the opportunity. A strong strategy, and one that could become a full-time focus in itself.

FUNDAMENTAL 7:
INVEST FOR THE LONG-TERM

Whilst there are many strategies in property, the three we're focusing on here are the time served, reliable, and most common strategies of buy-to-let, buy-to-flip, and trading.

When sourcing deals, you're generally going to run them through the mill.

You'll look at a deal, and you'll determine first and foremost if it is in fact a deal.

You'll ask yourself, "Is this a buy-to-let?"
You'll ask yourself, "Is this a buy-to-flip?"

You'll ask yourself, "Should I sell this on?"

You'll know the answers because you've made your rules, and you stick to them.

If you plan on building a portfolio for the long-term, either on it's own, or whilst flipping and trading along the way, cherry picking the best deals for your own longer-term focus, then you'll want to benefit from capital growth; the property going up in value over time.

So whilst you do this, I want you to think about something...

What's wrong with taking the property you purchased five years ago, and trading it on? Why can't both worlds, the long-term and short-term, merge?

If we cut the emotion from our deals, and look at building for the long-term, whilst trading for short-term cashflow, we can start to realise that even the deals we've had for some time, can be packaged and sold to release capital, providing the timing is right.

Fundamental 7 is to invest for the long-term.

Do that.

Cherry pick the best deals for yourself.

And if a time comes when you'd rather sell the property, or trade the deal; great, do it.

FUNDAMENTAL 8:
HAVE OR BUILD A CASH RESERVE

I'm sure you'll agree, there's nothing overly difficult about the fundamentals, right?

In fact, I hope you agree, that everything so far in this book, is reasonably straight forward?

Sure, there are some moving parts, and it may be new to you, but it's not difficult.

Our final fundamental, is to have or build a cash reserve.

When you start in property, you may not have cash set by. What I recommend you do, is take 10% of your monthly rental income, and set it aside in a separate account, to cover the 'what-ifs'. This includes boiler repairs, voids, and so on.

Trust me, things will come up that you don't see coming.

Your cash reserve will allow you to relax, and not worry about things like missed payments, taking out loans, or borrowing to cover costs. These are worst case scenarios that amateur investors find themselves in because they're spending all of their money and have no cash reserves set aside.

BUILDING YOUR PROPERTY POWER TEAM

Let's start with a story…

Once upon a time, a ship's engine had failed and no one could fix it. The team hired an engineer with 40 years of experience. He inspected the engine very carefully, top to bottom. After looking things over, the engineer reached into his bag and pulled out a small hammer. He gently tapped it, and instantly, the engine shuddered back to life.

Seven days later, the owners received an invoice for £10,000.
"Seriously?" the owners yelled.
"You hardly did anything. Send an itemised bill."
The engineer complied…
'Tapping with a hammer, £2.
Knowing where to tap, £9,998.'

The lesson: never underestimate the value of experience and expertise.

In the property game, you're going to need a team of experts on-hand to support you when called upon; we call this your Property Power Team.

When building your Power Team, you must never look for the cheapest options. You must look for experience and expertise from people in each profession. Naturally, we want a fair price, but as the saying goes, when you pay peanuts, you get monkeys.

If you want to fast-track your journey, avoid costly mistakes, make new connections, receive wisdom from those who've walked the path before you, and so on, then I suggest you go to work immediately on building your power team.

Now let's look at the professionals your team should consist of…

MORTGAGE BROKER

Having a Mortgage Broker who can work hard to find the best finance options to fit your situation is essential. You'll want a mortgage broker with access to the whole of the market, as well as commercial lending and bridging finance. To top it off, you'll want a broker who has strong relationships with business development managers of lenders. Relationships like this only happen if you have vast experience in the mortgage finance world. Having a strong relationship with the business development manager will mean that certain criteria can be overturned and adjusted in favour of certain cases. It's vital that your mortgage broker is someone who has the backbone to fight your corner, has the insight to think outside the box and who will communicate with you and keep you up-to-date with what's going on at all times.

CONVEYANCING SOLICITOR

Having a solicitor with a wealth of experience in dealing with your particular variety of property transactions is vital. The majority of conveyancing solicitors only know a narrow process; traditional residential mortgages and buy-to-lets. When the going gets tough with one of your deals and requires more input from your solicitor to get the deal over the line, you'll need someone who can get in the trenches and resolve your issues. You need a solicitor you can pick up the phone to and who can assist with potential pitfalls in your deals, and have them be able to tell you with absolute confidence and certainty whether a deal can be sorted or not, to avoid a commitment on your part to a bad deal.

ACCOUNTANT & TAX ADVISOR

In the ever-changing world of tax in relation to property, a strong accountant and tax advisor (preferably the same person or company) will save you a great deal of money and keep you on the right side of the line.

Having someone at the top of their game in this profession will allow you to stay on track, will allow you to keep more of your hard earned profits, and will give you the tax planning, structure, and foundational elements to build a strong business. More importantly, a strong accountant and tax advisor will remove the headache and allow you the freedom to build your empire.

LETTING AGENTS

As we've discussed at length, you'll need a proactive letting agent to ensure you let your properties fast, and achieve the best rent as well as securing good tenants. A strong letting agent will have a system in place to look after your property whilst keeping you updated. A strong letting agent will also give feedback on what you need to do in order to further enhance your property to maximise rental income as well as providing feedback on potential properties you may be looking as buy-to-lets.

The private rental sector (PRS) is constantly changing with more and more legislation being introduced. This serves not only to protect the landlord but the tenant too. With this in mind, a great letting agent should demonstrate that they are staying current and up-to-date with the relevant pre-checks that need to be carried out on both you as the landlord, and the tenant, as well as the property itself. Don't second guess this stuff, and please don't attempt to do this yourself. You must free up your mind in order to focus on your next deal, your next investor, or your next £100,000 investment into your property business. Leave the property management to the experts.

ESTATE AGENTS

When targeting a local market, it's wise to build relationships with some of the better local agents who know the market inside out and can guide and support you on a number of levels.

A good estate agent is someone who will be proactive in getting your flip properties sold, but more importantly, can give you free valuations and support when it comes to renovations, advising you on what homebuyers in that area are looking for. An estate agent wants to sell your property, so they will give you tips and pointers on how to do just that, as well as giving advice on which areas to buy and avoid buying in, if you're looking for a quick sale.

As you'll discover when you begin sourcing deals, there will be a whole number of leads that don't fit your criteria, but would be perfect for the open market, because the sellers aren't at the point of being overly motivated. This means you can pass referrals on to your preferred Estate Agent, and on the back of this, they're going to pass deals back to you that don't fit their criteria for the open market. This is reciprocation, helping one another. If the Estate Agent is going to source deals and they know that you're a developer, and that you're likely to buy property and put it back on the market with them, the chances are that they could give you first refusal on a number of deals.

With Estate Agents, it all comes down to relationships.

Don't attempt to meet and build relationships with every agent in town. Build some quality relationships with key Estate Agents, and preferably ones who know what they're doing.

BUILDERS (TRADESMEN)

As you'll be carrying out renovations, you'll need a builder.

When I say 'builder', I don't just mean one man, I mean a small building firm, and most definitely one that handles all of the trades that you'll ever need to carry out a job, at a reasonable rate, and to a high standard. Part of the reason why you'll want a builder who can handle all trades, is because having multiple tradesmen, plumbers, electricians, painters, roofers, etc on the same project, can become a bit of a headache to coordinate. You'll also be dealing with multiple people on different timescales.

You'll want a builder who has experience of doing buy-to-let and buy-to-flip renovations, so they'll know the importance of keeping costs down, and of what's required for the ideal finish. It's important that communication is on point, and in an ideal world, you'll have a relationship with your builder that allows you to hand over the keys, and know that by the time you get your keys back, the work will be complete, on budget, and on schedule as agreed.

You won't be hard pushed to find stories of rogue builders, and it can be quite off-putting to those just getting started. As property is such a small community in the UK, you'll ideally be looking for recommendations from those you meet at networking events, in peer groups, and so on. Even after receiving the recommendation, once you have your quote and the timeline on how long the renovation will take, you'll want to see a few testimonials, along with before and after pictures of previous work. If the Builder has ongoing renovations or renovations nearing completion, ask if you can view them to get a feel for how they do things and more importantly, what the end product and finish looks like in person, rather than observing pictures of the work.

When working with your Builder, you want to stay in control. Don't pay them the full fee in advance. Pay your Builders in small chunks as the job progresses. You will pay an initial fee to get them moving and allow them to buy materials to get started, and then pay them throughout the process. As the work comes to an end, you'd want to hold back between 10% and 20%, before checking the property to ensure everything has been completed to the standard you'd expect. If there are any snagging issues that need to be handled, then have them carried out first, before you release the last of the funds.

PROPERTY SOURCERS

You're in property, right?

Great, well surely it can't hurt to know other people in property.

It's a smart move to have as many property sourcers as possible on your contact list. More so, those who know what they're doing, and can come up with the goods.

There are many sourcers out there. You'll meet them at networking events and elsewhere. These people are sourcing investments, in just the same manner as you, albeit not all of them take the time to read a book like this, or attend the Property Protege ™ Intensive, and therefore, they may not have the necessary guidance and resources available that you do. Regardless, sometimes people come up with the goods, and when someone has secured a deal that ticks your boxes, you can choose to add it to your portfolio, or, if it ticks the boxes for a flip, you could take it on as a flip, or if you've spent time building an investor database and finding people who are looking for deals, you could act as a middle person between the person who sourced the deal, and one of your own investors, adding your own fee on top. For example, the Sourcer is selling their deal for £2,000, but as it happens, you have an investor who'd pay £4,000. Awesome, pay the Sourcer their £2,000, sell the deal, and keep the other £2,000.

This is cashflow 101.

The more money you have coming into your business, the better.

The quicker you get moving in the game, and the closer you stay to what you're learning here, the more you're going to spot opportunities to help others and generate income.

BANK MANAGERS

When starting a new company, you'd be wise to build a relationship with the Business Banking Manager of your local branch of whichever bank you choose. By doing this, you're more likely to be able to increase your overdraft to put some funds behind you. As it happens, at the onset of your business, many of our Property Proteges have structured powerful business plans detailing how they're moving forward, and have been given £20,000 overdrafts from the beginning. This is a great way to generate funds to put towards a purchase, a renovation, or marketing in order to generate leads.

As your interactions with the business banking manager increase, and they begin to see more money coming into your account, you'll find that loan facilities and overdrafts will be put your way, leading on to commercial or bridging finance for larger deals. That said, you won't have this access through your business bank if you don't start to develop the long-term relationship.

INVESTOR DATABASE AND PRIVATE INVESTORS

We mentioned earlier that the easiest way to profit in property, is to take on two roles…

Find the deals.

Find the money.

Let's not overcomplicate it.

Finding the deals, with the correct knowledge, which we'll discuss shortly, is something that most people can get their head around, but what really trips many newbies up, is the idea of finding money; the idea that people would fund them, or fund their flips, or their deals, and so on.

The reality is, finding the deals is simple, and so money.

It's important that you begin to think about buil database. On this database could be personal contacts, family members, work colleagues, business associates, acquaintances, people on social media, and so on. You'd be surprised how many people have savings, or pension funds available, or equity they can release, or an investment pot. And you'd be surprised how many investors are out there looking for a place to make their money work for the best return.

When your deals don't fit the criteria for your *own* portfolio, you could either raise finance through one or more of your investors to fund a flip, or sell the deal (trade) to another investor, and perhaps even manage the process for them for an additional fee.

There are others who will want to invest in you personally, and in your vision. On our Property Protege ™ programme we show you how to present a deal to an investor in such a manner that they end up backing *you*. Now, there's a question you want to ask yourself. Why should anyone invest in you? At Property Protege ™, we help people position themselves as authorities in the game, and how to package up and promote their business to investors in a way that sees them raising £50,000, £100,000 or £500,000. We've even had people achieve £1 Million from private investment for a 10% return on the investor's funds. In the grand scheme of things, 10% is a good return for the investor but thankfully low for you, meaning anything over and above is profit. If your strategy is buy-to-flip, you can very easily start to play in the bigger leagues and make real money.

A STRONG MENTOR

Through our programme, Property Protege ™, I always find it interesting to see what people believe can be accomplished in a 12-month period. Generally, people set annual goals that can in fact be achieved inside the first month.

Why? Because you don't know, what you don't know.

Having a strong mentor with a wealth of experience in property will allow you to fast-track your own journey. They will keep you on track, support you, advise you, and keep you from making mistakes that they themselves may have made or watched others make. A mentor is someone

.10 can open doors, who will hold you accountable, and who, more importantly, will help you become a much stronger version of yourself inside the game.

A mentor can often be seen as an unnecessary expense, but I can tell you from personal experience of investing £500k+ over the past 10 years in training and mentorship, and more recently having had a Billionaire mentor, my businesses have consistently grown, and my drive, vision, and ambitions have taken me to levels I never imagined possible.

YOUR PROPERTY POWER TEAM

We've detailed a number of players you'd want on your team. As your business grows, that team will expend into different areas again, but right now, it's important to begin building relationships with experienced professionals in the areas above. Choose wisely based on experience, expertise, and track record. Better yet, choose based on good old fashioned trusted word of mouth.

In property, the cost of not having the right professionals on your side can be devastating. It's likely that in your own life you've paid more money for items of higher quality that have lasted longer and likely given more value, despite the temptations of buying at a lower cost, with the real cost surfacing as reliability, longevity, quality and value. Short-term solutions and savings, can be the most expensive option by far, and can cause you the most trouble along the way. There will come a time when you need the right person or people to turn to. Make sure you have that guidance.

BONUS CONTENT

Visit YourPropertyJumpstart.com/bonus
for your secret bonus chapter, the Protege Deal Calculator,
and additional content and resources to support you
on your property journey

CHAPTER 4:
GOLDMINE AREA AND DUE DILIGENCE

This will be one of the shortest sections of the book...

But also one of the most important.

Knowing your target area inside out, and being able to conduct thorough due diligence before taking a deal forward are vital ingredients in property.

If you follow what I'm about to share, you'll know when a deal is a deal, or not.

Far too many amateur investors make mistakes because they let emotion take over, and find themselves caught up in an individual property, perhaps because it was their first property, or their Gran lived in the same building, or they feel like they'll never get another deal like it. When you act on emotion, you can end up buying a property, not realising there are underlying issues, or you buy in an area that doesn't suit your exit strategy.

We act based on facts; not on emotion.

There are many variables when it comes to due diligence, and if you don't do this properly, mistakes are bound to happen that could cost you further down the line.

That being said...

Although due diligence is extremely important, it's just as important not to overanalyse.

If the deal stacks up, then do the deal.

Either buy the property, or put it through another exit strategy.

There's no point in sleeping on it, or meditating to see if the numbers change. We take emotion out of the equation by doing the due diligence and letting the figures speak for themselves, and then when we have that reality presented to us, we don't overanalyse, we do the deal.

Now, let's discuss the five steps of thorough due diligence…

STEP 1:
IDENTIFY YOUR GOLDMINE AREA

Identifying your Goldmine Area is about mastering a small area, becoming the local expert, and being known as an authority in that area. If you do this, you're going to get deals, you're going to understand property values, you're going to instinctively know where and when you can add value, and what the end-values on properties will be.

When you're starting off in your Goldmine Area, it's best to start with a 1/2 mile to 1 mile radius, and truly master that little location. Once you've mastered it, you can start to increase to 2 miles, 3 miles, 4 miles, 5 miles, and further afield, going on to other locations and having several Goldmine Areas at any one time. When you expand your area, it can be as large as you want, but in the beginning, trim it down and keep it simple.

When selecting your Goldmine Area, there are a number of things you want to consider. Does the area have universities, schools and hospitals? Does the area have good local amenities such as shopping centres and transport links? Is the area going through re-development? Is the area a high rental demand location?

You'll also want to be in a location where there are lots of first-time buyers. If your strategy is to sell property on the open market, there are no better buyers than first-time buyers, quite simply because first-time buyers are looking for a property that's in walk-in condition. Very few first-time buyers will have the funds to renovate a property. They have their deposit, and that's generally it. Not only do they generally lack funds for the renovation, but they generally won't have a power team and builders in place to the standard and price that you, as a professional property developer, will do.

First-time buyers are also less likely to negotiate on price. If anything, they'll negotiate £1,000 to £2,000 and consider it a win, or depending on the market conditions, pay *over* the market value. First-time buyers also haven't gone through the property purchase process before, so they don't necessarily have the experience on negotiating on a property. They find themselves emotionally attached to a property that's in walk-in condition, and they'll put in their best offer.

STEP 2:
UNDERSTAND YOUR MARKET

In order to master your goldmine area, you must understand it. You must know what walk-in condition values of a 1-bed, 2-bed, and 3-bed property looks like. You must know the walk-in condition values of each type of property, including cottage flats, tenement flats, semi-detached, detached, mid-terrace, end-terrace, bungalows, and so on. Each type of property, 1, 2, and 3-bed values.

To know what walk-in condition looks like, you'll want to start spending some time on online portals such as RightMove and Zoopla, and start to identify walk-in condition from the pictures shown. You'll also want to go out and view local properties to get a feel for the standard of work that's been carried out to achieve walk-in condition.

As we've discussed, we don't want to *buy* properties in walk-in condition. We want to buy or trade properties that are in a distressed condition or need substantial work, in order to negotiate big discounts. But by knowing the marketplace to the level I'm suggesting, you'll begin to understand the standard of renovation required in order to achieve that top-end market value on the other side with a newly renovated walk-in condition property.

As well as knowing what walk-in condition properties look like, you'll want to be able to identify property prices for the various property types, as well as understanding the local market rent in the same way. To do this, on both fronts, I'd suggest you develop a healthy obsession, and spend up to 30 minutes per day on RightMove and other portals. You'll learn a great deal about your local area by spending time building your relationship with your preferred estate agent and letting agent. Your estate agent will fill in the gaps with sale values, and your letting agent with rent, including what you could expect for local housing payments for Housing Benefit tenants.

One step further is to speak to local surveyors who can give you an insight and 'desktop valuation' on what a property may value at. That being said, you don't want to take up all of their time. They may be open with advice and support you at the onset, but unless you're giving them business, it will not continue. Surveyors make money when they conduct proper valuations. So, to build relationships with surveyors, give them business now and then. This way, they will happily continue giving you support and advice as they are receiving business in return.

STEP 3:
SEARCH PROPERTY SITES

With the likes of the aforementioned RightMove, Zoopla, and other portals such as MousePrice, you have completely free access to research until your heart is content. As noted, if I were you, I'd be spending a good 30 minutes per day on these portals, studying the lay of the land, pricing, recent sales, rental figures, and so on. You also have the added advantage of being able to register for a free account on RightMove, where you can draw a map of your area and set up alerts, ensuring that you receive an email each time there is a new listing in your Goldmine Area. This will help you stay ahead of the game and be the professional, by setting up systems and schedules in order to see the deals before anyone else.

STEP 4:
CRUNCH THE NUMBERS

Do the figures stack up?

This is the key question.

When crunching the numbers, you'll see the possibilities for each potential exit strategy, and will be able to determine the best course of action.

Things you should be considering and taking into account include purchase price, stamp duty, renovation costs, mortgage interest rates, interest rates on refinancing, loan-to-value ratio, selling costs, end-value, rental income, letting agent fees, factor fees, building insurance, how long your money is left in the deal after you refinance (we'll cover this in the investment strategies chapters), and so on.

Once we have the figures, we can see what our positive cashflow looks like from the rental income, or what our profit looks like as a buy-to-flip to sell on the open market. Alternatively, if you're not in a position to buy, this is your groundwork for preparing a deal for an investor to purchase as a trade, as well as giving you all of the info you need in order for you to become confident when making offers on properties.

STEP 5:
KNOW YOUR EXIT STRATEGY

Do the numbers work?

Do the figures stack?

Does it fit your criteria?

Does it tick the boxes on your own rules?

Can you add it to your portfolio, or is it a flip?

Might it even be a deal you'd joint venture on?

Or is it a deal you'll package up for another investor (trading) to generate cashflow?

When the boxes are ticked, and a deal is a deal, whatever that deal may be...

YOU DO THE DEAL!

I cannot stress this enough...

If it's a deal, do not overanalyse.

Cut the emotion, and do the deal.

BONUS CONTENT

Visit YourPropertyJumpstart.com/bonus
for your secret bonus chapter, the Protege Deal Calculator,
and additional content and resources to support you
on your property journey

CHAPTER 5:
INVESTMENT STRATEGIES

If you've made it this far into *Your Property Jumpstart* ™, I applaud you.

Let's be real, most people give up before they get into the core of the material.

But you're here, well done (providing you didn't skip to this point. If so, go back to the start and take it all in.)

In this chapter, we're moving away from the foundations, and into investment strategies.

In this chapter in particular, we're going to focus on buy-to-let, and buy-to-flip. We'll do BTL and BTF together, as every time you source a deal, you'll want to look for either of these two exit strategies, and if a deal doesn't stack based on your *own* criteria, you'd still want to present it to a third party investor by showing them both exits. We'll be discussing trading (otherwise known as sourcing, or deal packaging) in detail in the next chapter.

The first thing you'll want to understand is your investment criteria.

We've discussed the importance of knowing your Goldmine Area, and of knowing the type of properties you'll be looking for in order to maximise profit. At this stage, if you're going down the buy-to-let route, you need to be clear on what it is you're looking to achieve in terms of positive cashflow. I'd suggest anything over £250 positive cashflow per month as being a great deal based on property valued at £100,000 or less. Increase that amount as the property value increases and so forth.

You'll also have to work out how long you'd want to wait until you get your funds out; in other words, the money you used to buy the property, and any associated fees. I'm going to show you a model where you can refinance after 6 months and pull out all of your money.

That being said, if you're leaving some money in the deal, then I'd recommend only leaving it in for a maximum of 12 months. If the boxes are ticked, then it's a great deal.

The important thing of note is that it's *your* investment criteria. It's about finding what works for *you*. Some people are happy with £200 monthly cashflow. Some people are happy to leave their funds in the deal for 12 months. Some people will leave their money in the deal for 24 or 48 months. Some people have no interest in refinancing whatsoever; they're happy with the lower purchase price, having added value, and leaving the property cash flowing at a higher amount because they choose not to refinance and increase the borrowings on the mortgage. It's all about what *you* want, and what works for *you*.

The model I'm about to show you will allow you to pull your money out, which then allows you to repeat the process again and again, buying new properties with the same funds every 6 months. The more funds you have to play with, the larger number of properties you can purchase this with. This is your long-term investment strategy; your buy-to-let strategy.

So let's talk about your shorter term strategy: buy-to-flip. My recommendation would be that the profit you should be looking for on each deal would be a minimum of £15,000 based on properties valued at £100,000 or less, once again increasing that as the property value increases too. You'd want a minimum of £15,000 for every £100,000 that the property sells for. So if the property is £200,000, then I'd say look for £30,000 profit. Again, your investment criteria might be to only make £10,000 profit as a flip, and that's perfectly fine too. I should also add that in most locations across the UK, you wouldn't be going for £200,000 properties at the low end, with the exception of areas with higher values, particularly in London, but even so, the same rules apply, and it's all relative.

For the remainder of this chapter, I'm going to walk you through some examples to help you understand how to work the numbers. Please do not get caught up with the low figures used. Remember the higher the value and the bigger the numbers only means you must adjust your investment criteria of what you want to achieve, based on property prices within your own Goldmine Area, regardless of where you are operating in the UK.

I must add, when dealing with motivated sellers, you'll be able to secure 25%+ below market value deals, but what we really need to focus on are the numbers. By doing this, instead of focusing on the size of the discount you're getting, you'll pick up more deals. This will become clear in the examples that follow. In our four case studies, we'll discuss the figures for buy-to-let, and also buy-to-flip.

Let's play with the numbers...

Be warned, this is going to get deep. I'd encourage you to take your time and get a full understanding of what follows. It may be difficult or uncomfortable at first, but it'll be second nature and easily understood in no time at all.

CASE STUDY 1

Let's imagine you've started your marketing campaign, and a seller gets in touch with you. The property is a 2-bed flat, currently valued at £70,000, but because you know your Goldmine Area and have done your due diligence, you know that it will value at £90,000 when renovated to walk-in condition.

The seller is leaving the country inside two months, the tickets are booked, and after the sale of their property falling through, they are desperate to find a buyer but cannot afford the luxury of listing with an estate agent and selling on the open market. You've made it your mission to help them.

The Purchase Price (PP) you've negotiated is £59,500.

The Below Market Value (BMV) discount percentage is 15%, which we know, after using our BMV calculation as previously discussed...

$$((PV - PP) \div PV) \times 100$$

So in this case:
- £70,000 (PV) - £59,500 (PP) = £10,500
- £10,500 ÷ £70,000 (Property Value) = 0.15
- 0.15 x 100 = **15% BMV**

So let's work through the numbers here…

You get a mortgage on this property at 75% loan-to-value. This means that the mortgage lender is giving you 75% of the purchase price, with the remaining 25% being your deposit.

75% of the Purchase Price is £44,625.

However, when you get your mortgage, there's generally an arrangement fee of around 3%, which can be paid upfront or added to the loan. I'd suggest you add it to the loan. With this being the case, your total borrowings amount to £45,963.75, which includes the 3% arrangement fee added to the loan.

Let's list the Acquisition Costs:
- Deposit (25% of £59,500): £14,875
- Renovation: £10,000
- Stamp Duty at 3% of Purchase Price: £1,785
- Legal Fees: £800
Total Acquisition Costs = £27,460

Note: At the time of print (2018) the 3% stamp duty is only applicable if the purchase price is £40,000 or above, so if you're able to negotiate the price to under £40,000, you would be exempt from paying stamp duty. Alternatively, if you purchase six or more properties as the one transaction when acquiring a portfolio, you would also be exempt of paying stamp duty.

Stamp Duty rates for additional home as follows:
- Stamp Duty Land Tax (SDLT) rates for England and Northern Ireland is 3% up to £125,000
- Land and Buildings Transaction Tax (LBTT) rates for Scotland is 3% up to £145,000
- Land Transaction Tax (LTT) rates for Wales is 3% up to £180,000

As you go over the listed purchase prices you will have an additional percentage to pay for each bracket.

So, the total funds required are £27,460

The remainder, comes from the lender.

Next, we look at our monthly expenses.

The biggest expense would be the mortgage payment. When you get a mortgage, your broker will tell you the interest rate. For this example, we'll say it's 4.5%. Let's work it out…

Multiply the mortgage (incl arrangement fee) by the interest rate: £45,963.75 (Mortgage Amount) x 4.5% (Interest Rate) = £2,068.36 This number, the £2,068.36 is the Annual Interest.

To work out our monthly interest-only mortgage payments, we divide our annual interest of £2,068.36 by 12 (12 months of the year) ,which gives us monthly payments of £172.36.

We then have other monthly expenses to factor in:
• Letting Agents fees (Normally 10% of rental income which is £600) - £60 per month.
• Building insurance - £15 per month.

So if we put it all together:
• Mortgage: £172.36
• Letting agent fee: £60
• Insurance: £15
Total monthly expenses: £247.36

So if your monthly rental income is £600, your monthly cashflow would be £352.64.

This is relevant to the first six months. Why? Because after six months you're going to do one of two things: you're going to look at either refinancing to pull your funds back out and keep the property as a buy-to-let. Or, you're going to look at the exit strategy as a buy-to-flip, and sell it on the open market.

The reason you need to wait six months, is because there is a 'six month guide' that most traditional high street lenders adhere too. This is set by the Council of Mortgage Lenders. Not all mortgage lenders do, but the majority will make you wait six months before you can sell or refinance unless you are selling to a cash buyer or if the purchaser is using a lender who does not adhere to the 6 month guide.

So, let's look at possible exit strategies for this deal…

EXIT STRATEGY 1:
Buy-to-let

We know the end-value of this property is £90,000, so as a buy-to-let, we're going to refinance at that amount. Once you've carried out the renovation work required, you'd get in touch with your mortgage lender to let them know you've added value to the property and want to refinance in the form of a 'further advance', increasing your borrowings to the new value of the property. They'll then send a Surveyor to value the property to make sure the property is worth the £90,000, and give the go-ahead to allow you to gain additional borrowings and to refinance to the new market value. In this case, you'd get 75% loan-to-value of £90,000. This works out at a new mortgage of £67,500 plus your arrangement fee of 3%, which takes your new mortgage to £69,525.

We now need to work out the new monthly interest payments.

£69,525 (Mortgage Amount) x 4.5% (Interest Rate) = £3,128.62

Divide this number by 12, and you have £260.72 as your new monthly payment.

We also still have our Letting Agents fee of £60, and building insurance at £15.

This gives us a new monthly expense total of £335.72

£600 (Monthly Rent) - £335.72 (Monthly Expenses) = £264.28 Positive Monthly Cashflow.

So let's look at how much you'll be able to pull out of the deal after refinancing…

The new mortgage amount is £67,500 (we don't include the arrangement fee here because the fee is added to the loan amount). The original loan amount was £44,625. If you take the original amount away from the new amount, we have a difference of £22,875. This is what the bank is going to release to you when you refinance the property after 6 months.

The total amount invested into the deal was £27,460

£27,460 (Total Invested) - £22,875 (Additional Funds from Refinance) = £4,585

This is how much you're leaving in the deal: £4,585

Now that you know the new monthly cashflow is £264.28, you simply divide the funds left in the deal by the cashflow, which in this example, gives us 17, meaning 17 months of positive cashflow and you then have an infinite return on your initial investment. If you're happy with this deal, and it ticks the boxes for your investment criteria, fantastic, add it to your portfolio.

EXIT STRATEGY 2:
Buy-to-flip

Let's say you didn't want to add this property to your portfolio, rather, you'd prefer it as a flip.

We'd need to work out all of the costs that need covered and paid back.

So, we know our Purchase Price is £59,500.

We know the mortgage amount is £45,963.75 (this amount includes the arrangement fee this time because when you're flipping the deal you have to pay the fee back once you sell the property).

We know the Total Cash Investment is £27,460

The Total Mortgage Amount of £45,963.75 + Total Acquisition Costs of £27,460 = £73,423.75

There are some additional costs still to be factored in for selling the property.

The selling costs we have to take into account include the Home Report or Valuation, which we'll say is £300. We'll have another set of legal fees because we're now going to sell the property, which we'll say are £800. We'll have estate agents fees, which we'll say are £1,000. And we have six months of mortgage payments due to holding the property for that initial time taking into consideration the six month guide set by the council of mortgage lenders. The initial mortgage payment of £172.36 x 6, which is £1,034.16

So, the total fees to sell the property come to £3,134.16

£3,134.16 (Selling Fees) + £73,423.75 (Total Costs) = £76,557.91

The £76,557.91 is the total amount we have to pay back from the sale of the property before we make any profit. We know the sale price is going to be £90,000, so…

£90,000 (Sale Price) - £76,557.91 (Total Costs) = £13,442.09 Buy-to-flip Profit.

So, again, what's your investment criteria?

Does this particular deal tick your boxes when you look at it as a buy-to-flip? Or is this one a buy-to-let? If neither work for you, then package it up and sell it to an investor, which we'll discuss soon.

CASE STUDY 2

In this example, I'm going to go a step further to show you the difference between buying a property for cash, and leveraging a mortgage on it. There are pros and cons to both which we will discuss later. Just remember, it's all about the numbers. As a company, we generally buy all of our properties cash, mainly due to the fact that we want to be in a position to move fast, but if you have limited funds then you might want to split your funds in order to do multiple deals. I like the idea of leveraging mortgages when funds are lower and this is exactly what I did for the first decade of my property journey, because you can make your money go further.

So let's take another scenario...

Your marketing is in full flow, and a seller approaches you through one of your leaflets. The seller is in financial difficulty. They've had their head in the sand, and now it's time to act. They've been ignorant to the details for so long that they don't have the time to sell the property on the market with an estate agent, and what was once their home, is now a burden that they wish to offload to pull some funds in.

In this example, let's say the end-value of this property is £85,000 walk-in condition.

The current Home Report and valuation on this property is £50,000.

The agreed Purchase Price is £55,500.

So in this case, you're actually paying £5,500 *over* the Home Report value.

Remember, if we ignore the discount (or lack thereof) for a moment, even though we always want to buy at discount, and focus on the numbers, I'll show you how you can offer over the valuation, and still tick all of the boxes for a buy-to-let or a buy-to-flip.

I'll save you the time of having to read through all of the notes used in example 1, by cutting straight to the chase on the numbers...

- Purchase Price: £55,500
- Renovation: £10,000
- Stamp Duty (3%): £1,665
- Legal Fees: £800
  Total Acquisition Costs = £67,965

It's important to know that lenders will typically lend you 75% of the purchase price *or* the valuation; whichever is lower. In this example, the purchase price is higher than the valuation, so the lender would only lend 75% of the valuation. This means, that you'd have to put the extra £5,500 on top of your deposit to get the deal.

So let's work it out...

The mortgage amount is 75% of £50,000, which is £37,500. When we add the 3% arrangement fee, we have £38,625. Your deposit of 25% works out at £12,500. We then add the additional £5,500, plus the renovation costs of £10,000, plus the stamp duty at £1,665, and the legals at £800, and we have our total acquisition costs at £30,465.

On the expenses side, we have our monthly mortgage payments, which work out at £144.84 (Mortgage Total multiplied by Interest Rate of 4.5% divided by 12 months). We also have our letting agents fee of let's say £60 (10% of our £600 rental income), and buildings insurance at £15, bringing our total monthly expenses to £219.84.

£600 rental income minus £219.84 expenses, is £380.16 positive monthly cashflow.

Let's look at our two exit strategies, plus a cash buy option.

EXIT STRATEGY 1:
Buy-to-let

Exit strategy possibility number 1, is buy-to-let.

If this were a cash buy (verses leveraging a mortgage), all you'd be doing is putting a mortgage on the property after six months; not refinancing. Again, with the six month guide in mind, most lenders will make you wait the six months to put a mortgage on the property even though you bought the property cash in the first place.

The mortgage route…

So, we're going to be refinancing at 75% of £85,000, which we know is the end-value. 75% of £85,000 is £63,750 + 3% arrangement fee gives you a mortgage amount of £65,662.50. That's your mortgage amount. Let's keep that at 4.5% interest rate to see what our new monthly payments will be. This gives us an annual interest of £2,954.81, divided by 12 gives us a monthly mortgage of £246.23.

So again, we add our monthly expenses. Our letting agents fee at £60, our building insurance at £15, and our new monthly mortgage amount at £246.23, with a total of £321.23.

So, £600 per month rent, less £321.23 expenses, gives a new monthly positive cashflow figure of £278.77. That's a big tick for the £250 per month cashflow I'd suggest you go after.

If you're trying to get the money out of the deal, then how much money are we getting out if we take it from the point of view of initially leveraging a mortgage…

The new mortgage amount is £63,750. The original mortgage amount was £37,500. If you take the original amount away from the new amount, we have a difference of £26,250. This is what the lender is going to release to you when you refinance the property.

The total amount invested into the deal was £30,465.

£30,465 (Total Acquisition Costs) - £26,250 (Additional Funds from Refinance) = £4,215.

This is how much you're leaving in the deal. £4,215.

With our monthly cashflow at £278.77, we'd simply divide the funds left in the deal by the cashflow, which in this example, gives us 15, meaning, 15 months of positive cashflow and you have an infinite return on investment. If it ticks your criteria, great, go for it. If it doesn't, and it also doesn't work as a buy-to-flip, then package it up and sell it on to another investor.

The cash purchase route…

Let's look at this from the point of view of a cash purchase, as a buy-to-let.

The total cash investment required, was £67,965. This included the purchase price, the renovation costs, legals, stamp duty, and other associated fees.

This means, that your cash back would be £67,965 (total initial investment) minus £63,750 (75% of the new value of £85,000), which gives you a total of £4,215 left in the deal. So in this case, there would be no benefit to buying cash as a buy-to-let. All you'd do here is tie up more money, therefore, a mortgage would be the better option in this example if you were going to go down the buy-to-let route.

EXIT STRATEGY 2:
Buy-to-flip

So let's say you've run the numbers, and you're looking at the potential of a buy-to-flip. First we'll look at the mortgage route, and then the route of buying cash.

The mortgage route…

Hopefully you're starting to get this now, so let's move swiftly.

Our mortgage plus the 3% arrangement fee, is £38,625. Add to this our total amount invested, at £30,465, and we're at £69,090.

We'll have to factor selling costs in too, for example, Home Report (or valuation) let's say £300. Legals at £800. Estate agency costs at £1,000. We also have our monthly mortgage multiplied by six months, which is £869.04. Our total selling fees are £2,969.04.

Now let's add our total selling fees to £69,090 (our mortgage and cash invested). £2,969.04 + £69,090, gives us £72,059.04. So, this is how much we have to pay back from the sale.

Our end-value, the sale price, is £85,000. Take our total mortgage and cash invested £72,059.04 away from our total end-value, and we have £12,940.96 profit as a buy-to-flip.

Again, this could be a great deal if it matches your investment criteria. Or, again, it could be a great deal for someone else, if it doesn't.

The cash purchase route…

Our total acquisition costs, were £67,965, which includes the purchase price (£55,500), the renovation (£10,000), 3% stamp duty (£1,665), and legal fees (£800).

We still have our selling fees to take into account. We have the Home Report and valuation at let's say £300, our estate agency costs at let's say £1,000, and legals at let's say £800. Our total selling fees, this time, are £2,100. We don't have any mortgage interest payments to account for as we are purchasing cash.

So, our total invested (£67,965) plus our selling fees (£2,100) is £70,065.

If we take our end-value (our sale price) of £85,000 and take away our £70,065 total invested plus selling fees, our profit on a cash buy is £14,935.

So hopefully you can see, that if you don't leverage a mortgage, and you have cash to buy the property, then you're going to save some money on the fees, and the monthly interest payments, and that's why the profit from this deal as a cash buy is slightly higher on this buy-to-flip. What I want to draw your attention to in this example which you may have missed however is vitally important is that we purchased this property *over* the current market value. This further illustrates the necessity to know your numbers and end-values and not to be caught up in the below market value percentage.

In this example we showed both leveraging a mortgage as well as buying cash. The benefit of buying cash is that it puts you in a strong position when it comes to negotiation and the speed at which you can buy. The purchase process with a cash buyer is a fraction of the time of someone leveraging a mortgage. Being able to purchase with cash isn't just about saving a few thousand in fees, it may be the difference in securing the deal in the first place when time is the deciding factor and the ability to move fast may come down to being a cash buyer.

That said, if time wasn't the deciding factor, leveraging a mortgage will allow you to make your working capital go further. In this same example the total acquisitions costs were £26,950 if leveraging a mortgage. If we had two similar deals going through at the same time that's a total acquisition cost of £53,900 which is still less than the total acquisition costs you would need to purchase the property in this example as a cash buy. If you leveraged a mortgage on two similar deals you will have made double the profit, rather than tying all of your funds up in just one deal. Providing you have time to utilise a mortgage, always leverage.

CASE STUDY 3

So, let's go a step further, and run the numbers on a 1-bed to 2-bed conversion.

You're about to see that you can add a great deal of value to a property if you can increase the space in the house to make an extra bedroom, put on an extension, or an attic conversion. When you start to understand your Goldmine Area, you'll see properties within the area that can easily be 1-bed to 2-bed conversions, or 2-bed to 3-bed conversions, or they're perfect for adding an extension.

Let me give you an example from one of my own deals…

Basically, we changed the layout to take it from a 1-bed to 2-bed flat, moving the kitchen to create the second bedroom, whilst also adding an en-suite to the master bedroom.

So for this area, we knew that the walk-in condition end-value of a two-bed flat was £95,000. The Home Report valuation on the property was £70,000. The property was actually in good condition. It needed a new kitchen and some general paint and decor, but that was the extent of it. If I'd added a new kitchen and instructed some basic decor, it would value at £80,000 for 1-bed flats in this particular area. So by changing the layout to make it a 2-bed flat, we were adding an extra £15,000 of value.

When it comes to renovation for conversions, you're going to have to get an architect involved to do the drawings for the new layout. You're going to need a structural engineer in some cases if something structural needs to be amended. You're also going to need to get your local council or authority to sign off on it, and give you the Building Warrant to allow the work to go ahead. You'll need to factor these extra costs into your figures. For this deal, we managed to secure the property at a discount, for £55,000, and our renovation totals came to £18,000. Even though the property was in good condition, we were changing the layout, which meant a new kitchen, a new bathroom, paint and decor, plus the extra costs for structural work and planning.

So let's look at the numbers, and then our exit strategies…

The mortgage. 75% loan-to-value of £55,000 is £41,250. Add on the 3% arrangement fee, and we're at £42,487.50. This is our mortgage amount.

- Deposit (25% of £55,000): £13,750
- Renovation: £18,000
- Stamp Duty (3%): £1,650
- Legal Fees: £800
  Total Acquisition Costs - £34,200

Taking the mortgage of £42,487.50, multiplied by a rate of 4.2% which gives an annual interest of £1,784.47, divided by 12 months, gives us a monthly mortgage payment of £148.71.

We then have monthly expenses, including the letting agency management fee (10% of the £550 per month rent) at £55, the building factor costs (such was the case with this particular property), building insurance at £25, and then we add the monthly mortgage payment of £148.71, giving us total expenses of £228.71 per month.

If we take our £228.71 monthly expenses from our £550 rent, our monthly profit is £321.29.

So let's look at our possible exits…

EXIT STRATEGY 1:
Buy-to-let

Let's imagine this is your own deal, and let's run it through as a buy-to-let.

So again, you're going to look at refinancing once you've carried out the renovation and converted it to a 2-bed. You've contacted the lender who will send a surveyor out, and they're now going to see it's a 2-bed property. They'll check the Building Warrant and make sure everything is in place and then revalue the property at the new market value of £95,000. This will then allow your lender to lend 75% of £95,000, which gives you the new mortgage amount of £71,250. Remember, we have to add on our 3% arrangement fee, which gives a total mortgage of £73,387.50.

Now let's work out the new monthly mortgage…

4.2% of £73,387.50 comes in at £3,082.27. Divide this by 12, and you have your monthly mortgage amount at £256.86.

So we have our total expenses, of letting agent at £55, factor fee at £25, and the new mortgage at £256.86, giving us total outgoings of £336.86.

Deduct our £336.86 expenses from our monthly rent of £550, and our monthly cashflow after refinancing is £213.14.

Does this tick the boxes for your investment criteria?

If not, check to see if it works as a buy-to-flip, or package it up and sell it to an investor.

Let's see how much money we pull out of the deal. We have the new mortgage amount of £71,250 minus the existing mortgage amount which we know was £41,250, giving us a total of £30,000 cash out. So when you refinance, the mortgage lender is going to send you that £30,000.

The cash invested, was £34,200, covering the deposit, stamp duty, legals and renovation. If we take away our £30,000 cash back amount, we have £4,200 left in the deal. If we take the £4,200 and divide it by the new positive cash flow of £213.14, it'll be 19 months before you've gotten all of your money out of the deal. It doesn't tick our boxes for my recommended 12 months, however does it tick your *own* investment criteria for a buy-to-let? If not, let's check if it ticks the boxes as a buy-to-flip.

EXIT STRATEGY 2:
Buy-to-flip

- Our end-value is £95,000
- The purchase price is £55,000
- Our mortgage + 3% arrangement fee is £42,487.50
- The total amount invested, is £34,200
- So, the mortgage, plus funds invested, totals at £76,687.50

Our selling costs, including the Home Report or valuation at £300, plus legals at £800, estate agency costs at £1,000, and 6 months of monthly mortgage payments at £892.26, gives us our total selling costs of £2,992.26.

Add our total mortgage and funds invested to our selling costs, and we're at £79,679.76.

The sale price, is £95,000. Take away our costs at £79,679.76 and our profit in the deal is £15,320.24 as a buy-to-flip.

Does this tick the boxes for your investment criteria? Or will you package this up and sell it on to other investors?

Some people would be happy with the buy-to-let model and would happily wait the 19 months for an infinite return on their investment. Others would be happy with the cashflow as they're not looking to refinance the property.

Now, let's look at one more example.

Let's look at the type of deals you'll pick up once you truly play this game to win. These are the type of deals I would never have thought possible until I got serious and kicked off my own marketing, which we'll discuss soon.

CASE STUDY 4

First of all, congratulations if you're still reading; I know this can be heavy.

The potential results off the back of this mentally taxing activity, however, are what makes it all worth it. If you're still here, chances are you'll get to enjoy what many others won't.

The following example is typical of deals that you will get when you are consistent with your marketing, and when you're following all of the principles shared in this book. Providing you apply what you're learning, six months from now you will likely be a completely different person in your capabilities. Knowledge when acted upon, compounds. It's in the doing of the work, where the magic happens.

Let's say a motivated seller gets in touch with you, due to your consistent marketing efforts. They find themselves in a situation where they're about to be repossessed, as they have fallen behind on their mortgage payments and are days away from having a repossession order approved, meaning they'll be evicted. You step in and are able to act fast and stop the repossession, as you've worked the numbers and know you have a buyer for the property. In this particular case, the buyer will be you, as it ticks all of your investment criteria boxes.

Let's dig into the details…

You know the area well, and you know that the walk-in condition end-value of this 3-bed detached house is £150,000, however, the property is in very poor condition and requires a full renovation. In its current condition, it would value at £100,000. In order to bring the property value up to £150,000, you would have to replace the kitchen, the bathroom, the en-suite, the windows, and the electrics, as well as plastering most walls and ceilings, painting and decorating throughout, and new floor coverings as well as tidying the overgrown garden. Basically, it needs a full renovation that will total £25,000.

After meeting with the seller to discuss their financial situation and what's outstanding, the seller has to receive £77,000 just to clear their mortgage and arrears. The seller wants to avoid being repossessed as they know by doing so, they won't be able to get another mortgage for a very long time. After working out the numbers, let's say you're able to negotiate a 20% discount below the current market value. This would then clear the seller's outstanding mortgage, and pay off the arrears to allow for a clean sale, as well as giving the seller £3,000 to get back on their feet.

So let's look at the numbers, and then our exit strategies...

The mortgage. 75% loan to value of £80,000 is £60,000. Add on the 3% arrangement fee, and we're at £61,800. This is our mortgage amount.

- Deposit (25% of £80,000): £20,000
- Renovation: £25,000
- Stamp Duty (3%): £2,400
- Legal Fees: £800
  Total Acquisition Costs = £48,200

The total mortgage amount of £61,800, multiplied by a rate of 4% in this example, gives us an annual interest of £2,472, divided by 12 months, gives us a monthly mortgage payment of £206.

(You will notice that throughout these examples the mortgage interest rate has changed slightly. The reason for doing this is to help you understand and become familiar with the different rates that you will be offered by your mortgage broker.)

We then need to work out our total monthly expenses, including the letting agency management fee (10% of the £850 per month rent) at £85, building insurance at £25, and then we add our monthly mortgage payment of £206, which gives us a total of £316 in monthly expenses.

If we take our £316 monthly expenses from our £850 rent, our monthly profit is £534.

So let's look at our possible exists…

EXIT STRATEGY 1:
Buy-to-let

So let's imagine this is your own deal, and let's run it through as a buy-to-let.

So again, just as in the previous examples, you're going to look at refinancing once you've carried out the renovation. You've contacted the lender who sends a surveyor out, and they revalue the property at the new market value of £150,000. This then allows your lender to lend 75% of £150,000, which gives you the new mortgage amount of £112,500. Remember we have to add on our 3% arrangement fee, which gives a total mortgage of £115,875.

So let's work out the monthly mortgage…

4% of £115,875 comes in at £4,635. Divide this by 12, and you have your monthly mortgage amount at £386.25.

We also have our expenses, with the Letting Agent at £85, and building insurance at £25. Add on our new mortgage payment at £386.25, and we have total monthly outgoings of £496.25.

Deduct our £496.25 in monthly expenses from our monthly rent of £850, and our monthly cashflow after refinancing is £353.75.

Does this tick the boxes for your investment criteria?

It not, check to see if it works as a buy-to-flip, or package it up and sell it to an investor.

Let's see how much we pull out of the deal. We have our new mortgage amount of £112,500, minus the existing mortgage amount which we know was £60,000, giving us a total of £52,500 cash out. So when you refinance, the mortgage lender is going to send you that £52,500.

The cash invested, was £48,200, covering the deposit, stamp duty, legals, and renovation. In this case, the cash back from the further advance is greater than your acquisition costs, meaning you will have actually had cash out of £4,300, meaning not only did you cover all of your acquisition costs, but you made a profit of £4,300, so now have zero of your own money left in the deal after refinancing in six months. I'm sure you will agree that this deal ticks both the monthly cashflow box as well as the time it takes to get all of your working capital out of the deal.

Now, even though you'd likely add this deal to your portfolio, let's still run the numbers to see what you would make as a buy-to-flip, as your current focus may be on short-term strategies to give you the maximum income to allow you to go full-time in property as quickly as possible.

So let's run the numbers again…

EXIT STRATEGY 2:
Buy-to-flip

- Our end-value is £150,000
- The purchase price is £80,000
- Our mortgage + 3% arrangement fee is £61,800
- The total amount invested, is £48,200
- So, the mortgage, plus funds invested, totals £110,000

Our selling costs, including the Home Report or valuation at £500, plus legals at £800, plus estate agency costs at £1,500, and six months of monthly mortgage payments at £1,236, gives us our total selling costs of £4,036. Add on our total mortgage, and funds invested, and we're at £114,036.

(Side note, you'll notice that the Home Report in this example is more than the previous examples. What you will find is that when the value of the property increases so does the cost of the Home Report or Valuation Report.)

The sale price, is £150,000. Take away our costs at £114,036, and our profit in the deal is £35,964 as a buy-to-flip.

Does this tick the boxes for your investment criteria as a buy-to-flip? Absolutely…

The tough decision with this deal, is whether to add it to your portfolio, or to flip for the profits now. If your goal and focus is to be a full-time property investor or developer, one deal like this could very well be all it takes to allow you to do so. Bank that £35,964, and pay yourself a monthly wage of £3,000, then get to work on finding the next deal.

It's been a deep chapter for sure.

We've covered four different case studies.

We've discussed buy-to-let and buy-to-flip.

We've discussed cash purchases against mortgages.

We've discussed paying over the current market value, and still negotiating a deal and making extra profit through adding more value.

We've shown you the types of deals that will come your way over time, and how you can cash out on the deals after refinancing.

Well done for making it to this point.

I'd encourage you now to take some time to pull the numbers apart. Play with the figures, run some examples with other numbers, and get a true grasp and feel for this.

BONUS CONTENT

Visit YourPropertyJumpstart.com/bonus
for your secret bonus chapter, the Protege Deal Calculator,
and additional content and resources to support you
on your property journey

CHAPTER 6:
PROPERTY TRADING AND DEAL PACKAGING

Deal packaging, or property trading, is essentially the selling of deals. You're trading the deal opportunity without actually owning the property yourself. You are the bridge, the middle-person, between the person selling the property, and the investor.

This particular strategy is what allowed me to get started in property, and is what allowed me to get cash behind me, to take the jump to going full-time in property. It's been a consistent winner over the past 10 years, and has made me a great deal of money. This is one of the first things we teach at Property Protege ™, as it gives the fastest possible means to making serious income through property, allowing many of our Proteges the freedom to choose how to spend their time.

For most people, the idea of getting started in property usually involves creating financial freedom through holding property (buy-to-let) and earning from the monthly rental income. The challenge with this is if your financial freedom number is even as low as £2,000 to replace all of your own monthly expenses, and each property makes you an average of £250 per month positive cashflow, you're going to need eight properties to achieve this number. This doesn't take into account void periods, repairs or maintenance costs which eat away at your cashflow, and trust me, these issues will arise.

A portfolio of eight properties is going to take time to build, and you're going to be restricted by the level of finance available to you at the onset of your property journey. If you only have a small pot of cash, for example enough to purchase one property, which you'd then look to pull out your initial investment and roll into the next deal as we've discussed, you'd only have enough to do two properties per annum.

Of course, the more money you have, the more properties you can buy, but by focusing on deal packaging, you can reach that financial freedom figure even faster, creating freedom, and the ability to focus on property full-time, allowing you to create cash now, and build your portfolio later.

This was the route I chose.

To be fair, I didn't choose it; it's all I was able to do at the time.

It turned out to be a phenomenal move.

I focused on sourcing the deals, negotiating the discounts, and structuring win-win scenarios for all involved. I built relationships with investors, and sold them my deals, whilst simultaneously building relationships with estate agents to get their off-market properties, which I'd also then sell onto investors. Each time I sourced a deal with a purchase price less than £100,000, I was taking a minimum of £2,500 as a fee for packaging the deal.

So with that in mind, working with the low end fee of £2,500 (low end because I'm going to show you how to take two to three times that number), you could either buy eight properties with £250 per month cashflow, or to achieve a financial freedom figure of £2,000 (as per our example), you could source one property that ticks the boxes for an investor, and make even more. Wouldn't it make sense to focus on packaging deals in the first case? Imagine sourcing two or three per month at our low end £2,500. As you begin to implement your own marketing strategies, whilst building relationships with local agents, understanding your local area, raising finance, practicing negotiation, and so on, you will easily be able to secure one deal per month, and as you continue, that can very quickly rise to two, and three per month. This is where you can create fast and predictable cashflow for your property business.

What's even more exciting about deal packaging, is that it's possible to do this on 10 to 15 hours per week, alongside your full-time employment or business. With this being the case, just imagine what could be possible when you create the opportunity to commit to full-time hours in property.

"Full-time in property Paul? But I don't even own any properties?!"

That's the point.

The quicker you reach your financial freedom figure, the quicker you'll be able to put 40, 50, 60 hours per week in, if you choose to. If you're putting that amount of time into your business, then you're going to source a lot more deals. Then, you're going to be taken more seriously by estate agents and other professionals within the industry, because they see you as a full-time property professional. You're going to be doing 3, 4, and 5+ deals per month, making over £10,000 per month just by packaging deals and following the process that I'm about to cover.

We've established that deal packaging can generate rapid cashflow, and it's the perfect strategy for those who don't have the funds to buy. By creating cashflow, you can very quickly find yourself in a position to fund your first buy-to-let or buy-to-flip, if you choose to do so, and the more time you spend honing your skills, the faster you'll be able to source and identify bigger opportunities, and deals that you would be mad not to cherry-pick and keep for yourself.

It's my favourite strategy. It's a strategy I focus on heavily with our Property Proteges to provide them with the tools and resources to go full-time in the fastest time possible, providing they put in the work. Hopefully now you see why, and how, this is possible.

So we know the benefits, now let's cover the four stages of deal packaging.

STAGE 1:
THE FACT FIND

Stage 1 is about qualifying the seller; gathering enough information so that we can move onto the other steps where possible, and prepare deals for the right exit strategy; be that buying for your own portfolio, or as a flip, or to sell as a packaged deal.

Essentially, you're gathering certain information from the seller.

The seller will generally come to you through your property sourcing website, or through various other forms of marketing, or through an estate agent or local contact. When they do, your job starts at stage 1, gathering information.

You'll want to know information regarding the property and their situation. You'll want to address the reason they're selling, the outstanding mortgage, and if there are any arrears or secured loans.

You'll also want to establish, without directly asking, how motivated they are.

If you're dealing with the seller directly, which as a sourcer doing your own marketing, nine times out of ten you will be, you can be open with them and let them know that you need this information so that you can structure a deal that works for all involved. More importantly, from your point of view, when you get a buyer in place, you won't want them to find out further down the line that the price agreed can't be accepted because the finance that's on the property is much higher. So, explain to the seller at this stage that you need to find out more about their financial situation. Let them know and reassure them that you're not out to offer at the lowest possible price, but you're simply fact-finding to establish the best scenario for them, for you, and for the buyer.

Once we have the information we require, we want to seek a form of commitment. We need to get them to jump through a hoop or two to make sure they are in fact, motivated. If you get a seller who doesn't do anything that you suggest, then that would strongly suggest that they're not motivated.

Seeking commitment could simply be having them take and send a few additional photographs of the property, or to simply arrange for you to have a viewing of the property. This simple little thing is a form of commitment as you now know you have someone keen to sell, who's looking to take it a stage further, and who won't waste your time.

Take the fact-finding process one step at a time. Your sourcing process, your website, your marketing materials, will ask for basic information such as what's your name, where's the property and why are you selling, but this is only enough to get them to the next point, where you'd pick up the phone, or go and meet them, and build rapport in order to continue the fact find.

STAGE 2:
DUE DILIGENCE AND ANALYSE THE DEAL

Earlier in the book, we discussed due diligence, so I'll keep this brief.

Once you've taken the information gathered in Stage 1, you'll use that information, coupled with your own knowledge of your Goldmine Area, local values, renovation projections, and so on. All to work out whether the opportunity is a deal or not. The more information you can gather in Stage 1, the easier this part of the process will be. What's the level of discount? Can you add value? Do the figures stack? Is it a deal? What will your offer be? Is there too much debt on the property when compared with what you're able to offer? What exit strategies are viable? When you do your due diligence, and you know your game, all of which we've discussed up until this point, you'll be able to know if it's a deal or not.

STAGE 3:
CLOSING THE DEAL

You've gathered the information.

You've conducted your due diligence and analysed the deal.

You now know where you stand, and what you can offer.

Stage 3, is when you'll find yourself back on the phone or in person to negotiate the purchase price, using our principles of negotiation to close the deal. It's important at this stage to set their expectations, to let them know what to expect as they move through each part of the sale process.

You'll then want the seller to sign what's known as a Lock-Out Agreement, which is essentially a Head of Terms to state that the seller has agreed to the purchase price you've offered, and which binds them to selling only to you inside a given period. I'd suggest three months. From your perspective, this protects your deal, which you have sourced and analysed, and also protects you in terms of the time you've put in, and your financial input. From the seller's perspective, it gives them peace of mind knowing they have a sale agreed.

STAGE 4:
SUBMIT TO INVESTORS

When you first get started, you may not have an initial list of investors. That's ok. That's what networking is for, to allow you to start to meet other investors and other Deal Packagers. If you have a deal, and it's a genuine deal, there will be people out there who'll take it from you. Naturally, you'll want to build your own little database of investors, as opposed to selling through another Deal Packager, to ensure you achieve 100% of the income from selling the deal. It's important to note, that even if you have 500 people on an investor database, generally, what I've found over time, is that a handful of people will be repeat buyers, and the rest won't amount to much. You'll find a number of people who trust you, who like you, and who are ready to buy. So, you don't need hundreds of potential buyers on your list. You simply need a handful of credible people who are ready to pull the trigger. At Property Protege ™ we teach multiple strategies for growing your investor database, inside and outside of the property communities with ease, but take note here, if you have a genuine deal, someone will take it.

So let's say you have a list of investors. When you have credible buyers, you'll likely pick up the phone, but let's say for now that you're sending an email.

On the email, you'll include the investment highlights; the cashflow as a buy-to-let, the expenses, the profit as a buy-to-flip, how long funds will be left in the deal, and a little bit of information about the location and the property type. At this stage, we're not giving all of the information to the investors; we're just giving them the highlights to find out their level of interest.

Once you get responses for more information, it's time to qualify your potential investors. Find out if they have the finances in place. Find out if they have cash, if it's a cash buy. Find out if they want to go ahead with it, and most important, are they prepared to put down a reservation fee. Before they do that, however, you're going to have to send additional information on the property, and perhaps a Home Report or valuation if there is one in place. You'll want to send additional photographs, and perhaps a video walkthrough, as some of your investors won't be able to physically view the property, and the additional information will help the investor come to their decision.

Once you've sent everything to the investor, it's time to follow up. When they're interested in moving forward, you'll want to take a reservation fee (a commitment fee). A commitment fee is normally 50% of your full fee. You then take the other half on completion of the sale of the property. If you want to take the full fee upfront and if the investor is happy to do so, there's no reason why you can't. As you grow in confidence, this is what you'll likely do anyway. You can state a condition on the deal is that if the property falls through due to a fault from the investor's finances, that they lose their commitment fee, but if the sale falls through from the seller's side, you'll refund the investor in full. Now, if it falls through from the investor's side but the investor has done everything in their power to try to get the deal to go through, then you may want to refund them, as you'll want them to come back in the future to purchase additional deals. If, however, they've wasted your time, strung the process out, made it difficult for you to do the deal, and that's why it's fallen through, as the seller couldn't wait any longer, then I wouldn't recommend you return the fee.

So there you have it. The four stages of deal packaging:
- Find the deal and gather information.
- Work the numbers.
- Close and secure the deal.
- Sell the deal to another investor and facilitate the deal.

It's not rocket science; it's fairly straight forward.

PREFERRED INVESTORS VS INVESTORS

There's a huge difference between a preferred investor and an investor. I created the term 'preferred investor' primarily due to them being the type of investor you'd want and prefer. So what's the difference?

An investor is someone like yourself. They want the biggest discounts. Most of the time they begrudge paying a finder's fee. They don't want to utilise your power team; instead choosing to use their own. They are not loyal to you. As soon as they have taken a deal from you, they are out there taking deals from others. Investors will try to further negotiate your fee and sometimes try to further reduce the purchase price that you have agreed with the seller. They will try to take full control of the deal, which means you lose control, which could jeopardise your income.

On the other hand, a preferred investor is someone who wants to buy property to either build their portfolio, or to buy-to-flip, but they don't have the time, or perhaps they don't have the team, or the knowledge, whereas, you do. With this in mind, they need you to assist them in reaching their investment goals. They are looking for your expertise on where to buy and what type of properties they should be buying. More importantly they are looking for someone who can hold their hand throughout the process, and bring the power team to the table to help with all aspects, from arranging mortgages, conveyancing, managing builders and renovations, to instructing letting agents and estate agents. They are tapping into not only you, but your entire team, meaning you keep full control and make additional income from your power team in the form of referral fees. You'll want to make sure you can work with this type of investor, as your job as a Deal Packager means control is vitally important, from start to finish.

Preferred investors are also loyal. They will be repeat clients who will look to you to assist them in achieving their financial and property goals. The most important reason that you want to work with preferred investors is that they are not caught up on the big discounts nor the fact that you are being paid for sourcing the deal. They think very differently, seeing a 10% discount, or even less, as a great deal. Preferred investors focus on the returns, and your job is to structure the deal to suit all involved. They will look for smaller profits on flips, and they are not, in most cases, looking to pull all of their funds out of the property when refinancing a buy-to-let.

A preferred investor will make you a lot of money on the deals that neither you nor other investors would be likely to take. This is the low hanging fruit, when you can secure deals that other investors would turn their noses up at. They can still be great deals for someone, and that someone is your preferred investor.

The key is to educate your preferred investors, not in advanced strategies and the complex intricate details, but on why they should be investing in property, how it's a far greater pension, how it can help bring in additional income, and so on. You will handle their objections on what's held them back from getting started, and then give them the confidence to move forward, with you by their side to answer their questions and assist them in building wealth. By doing this, you will be creating loyal clients that will continue to buy properties from you, and will also pass referrals to you in the form of other clients. Property trading is the best business in the world when you are working with preferred investors.

THE DEAL PACKAGER'S ROLE

A property finder can source a deal, sell it to the investor, take their fee, and walk away. But a Deal Packager's role is much more involved. You're going to be involved through each step of the process until completion. You're going to be liaising with the seller, keeping them in the loop through the entire process, managing their expectations, answering their questions, and being their guiding hand.

You're going to liaise with the buyer, and make sure their finance is going through, get them to conclude missives or contracts, and get them to move forward as fast as possible.

You're going to liaise with the mortgage broker; the seller's and the buyer's. In some cases, until the deal completes, you're going to have to cover the seller's legal costs, so it becomes your responsibility to chat with the seller's solicitor, whom you've instructed for them, as well as the buyer's solicitor to make sure that everything goes as smoothly as possible and the property is sold within a timely manner.

The Deal Packager's role doesn't end when you've found the investor. You need to walk them through the whole process from start to finish and ensure everything is done, all of the boxes are ticked, and each person and moving part is managed along the way.

There's a reason why we find ourselves more involved than simply sourcing and selling deals, which will become apparent shortly.

STRUCTURING THE DEAL

Whilst discussing deal packaging, we've suggested the deal sourcing fee at being around £2,500. However, it can be more than that. It can also be less. It all depends on who your investor is, what the deal looks like, and what they're willing to pay for it.

Most property sourcers are missing out on making substantial income by simply not structuring the deal in the correct manner. They are leaving so much money on the table it's frightening. The majority of deal sourcers out there who focus on selling to investors as opposed to preferred investors, are lucky if they make £2,500 as a front-end finder's fee, and almost all of them won't make anything more than that. I'm going to show you how to include a back-end fee as a Deal Packager, that could double that amount. I'm going to give you an example, showing you how you should be making money from the front-end as well as the back-end, and money throughout the deal…

In this example, let's say you have secured a preferred investor, whom you have qualified, and they are looking to do the buy-to-flip strategy. Let's take a property that has an end-value of £85,000 after carrying out a renovation, however the market value in its current condition is £70,000. Let's say you're able to secure this for only 15% below the current market value which would be £59,500.

Now, you have secured this property at 15% below market value with the seller. However, the way we are going to structure this deal, is that we're going to offer it to our preferred investor for 10% below market value, which would make the purchase price £63,000. The agreed purchase price with the seller at 15% below market value is £59,500, and with 10% below market value discount, your delighted preferred investor is receiving, you are left with a back-end fee of 5%, which comes in at £3,500.

Not only do you have a back-end fee of £3,500, you have your front-end fee of £2,500, and you will have made a minimum of £250 in the form of commission from both the seller's and the investor's solicitors. You will have made a commission of £250 from the mortgage broker for arranging the mortgage, another £250 from the estate agent who will be marketing the property, and 10% commission from the builder's quote of £7,500 which comes in at £750. That's a total of £1,750 from commissions through referral fees as a result of using your power team.

- Front-end Sourcing Fee: £2,500
- Back-end Selling Fee: £3,500
- Commissions from Power Team: £1,750
  Total Deal Packaging Income = £7,750

This is more than three times the amount that a deal sourcer would typically make, when not structuring the deal in the correct manner.

Now I know what you're thinking. Why on earth would someone buy this deal? Well, let's look at what the preferred investor is set to make…

Property Purchase Price of £63,000

75% Loan to Value Mortgage + 3% Arrangement Fee: £48,667.50

Acquisition Costs as follows:

- Deposit (25%): £15,750
- Renovation Cost: £7,500
- Stamp Duty (3%): £1,890
- Legal Fees: £800
  Total Acquisition Costs = £25,940

Selling Costs as follows:

- Legals: £800
- Home Report (valuation): £350
- Estate Agency Fee: £750
- 6 Months Mortgage Repayments (4.5% Int Rate): £1,095
  Total Selling Costs = £2,995

Mortgage Balance of £48,667.50 + Acquisition Costs of £25,940 + Selling Costs of £2,995 = £77,602.50

New Market Value after the renovation of £85,000 - Total Selling Costs of £77,602.50 = £7,397.50 profit.

ROCE (Return On Capital Employed):
(Sold Price - Expenses - £7,397.50) ÷ (Acquisition Costs of £25,940) x 100 = 28.5%

That's a 28.5% return on their capital invested!

Now tell me again why someone wouldn't want to take this deal with a six month turnaround?

This is a deal that you secured at only 15% below the current market value, and that you offered to your investor for only 10% below market value.

Let's take the exact same example, however let's say you only secured this deal at 10% below the current market value, and you offered it to the preferred investor at only 5% below the market value. This means the seller would have agreed a purchase price of £63,000 and you would be selling the same deal to your preferred investor at a purchase price of £66,500.

- Front-end Sourcing Fee: £2,500
- Back-end Selling Fee: £3,500
- Commissions from Power Team: £1.750
  Total Deal Packaging Income: £7,750

You still make the EXACT same amount of money as you would have in the first example. There is zero loss to you as the deal Sourcer.

Let's look at what the preferred investor is set to make.
Property purchase price of £66,500
75% LTV Mortgage + 3% Arrangement Fee = £51,371.25

Acquisitions Costs as follows:

- 25% Deposit Required: £16,625
- Renovation Cost: £7,500
- 3% Stamp Duty of Purchase Price: £1,995
- Legal Fees: £800
  Total Acquisition Costs: £26,920

Selling Costs as follows:

- Legals: £800
- Home Report (valuation): £350
- Estate Agent Fee: £750
- 6 Months Mortgage Repayments (4.5% Int Rate): £1,155.84
  Total Selling Costs = £3,055.84

Mortgage Balance of £51,371.25 + Acquisitions Costs of £26,920 + Selling Costs - £3,055.84 = £81,347.09

New Market Value after the renovation of £85,000 – Total Selling Costs of £81,347.09 = £3,652.91 Profit

ROCE (Return On Capital Employed):
(Sold Price - Expenses - £3,652.91) ÷ (Acquisition costs of £26,920) x 100 = 13.5%

That's a 13.5% return on the preferred investors capital invested, in just a six month period. If the preferred investor had released equity from their own home at a rate of 3% per annum on this deal alone, they would have made 10.5% return on borrowed funds from the equity on their home. If they did a second flip in the following six month period to make the same, that's a 27% return on their money, less the 3% cost of the borrowings, giving your preferred investor an annual return on their money of 24%.

Average property investors would turn their nose up at the first example of this deal, let alone the second. It's all about perspective and showing your preferred investor the percentage return they will earn, as opposed to getting caught up in the below market value discount and making tens of thousands in profit. Those deals are the deals you are going to keep for yourself. Go for the low hanging fruit and, as per this example, you will have made £7,750 for yourself on a single deal. Source this same preferred investor two like-for-like properties in the same year, structured in this manner, and give yourself an income of £15,500 through just *one* client, sourcing only *two* properties that didn't match your own investment criteria.

Now tell me again how it's difficult to become a full-time property investor and become financially free on just a few hours per week.

OTHER INVESTMENT STRATEGIES

In *Your Property Jumpstart* ™, we've focused on two investment strategies: buy-to-let and buy-to-flip, as well as the all-powerful deal packaging strategy. But there are many other investment strategies available to you, including HMO's (house of multiple occupation), multi-lets, serviced accommodation, rent-to-rent, delayed completions (a phenomenal strategy that can allow you to own your dream home many years in advance), and options (albeit you can no longer do lease options in Scotland). You can follow our first-time buyer strategy, where if a first-time buyer buys right (whether that's you, or someone you're helping through it), within a five to ten-year period, they can have a couple of hundred thousand pounds sitting there, to either: pay off their mortgage; put towards a bigger mortgage; or just buy a property outright.

There's also 'title splitting', where you buy the property and split the title to turn it from one property into a number of properties. There's commercial-to-residential where you'd turn commercial premises into residential properties. There's new build development, where you'd acquire or secure land, and take it right through as a new build development, or secure the land, take it through planning, and then get the deal sold. There's also one of my favourites, 'assisted sales', where you'd joint venture with the seller and potentially make a great deal of money with nothing more than the renovation costs and the structuring of the deal.

There are many options available, so why have we focused on just a few?

Because I want you to get liquid as fast as possible.

I want you to put as much money in your pocket as fast as possible.

I want you to master the entry level content as fast as possible.

My own initial wealth came from three things: buy-to-let; buy-to-flip; and deal packaging.

Many cleverly named and well marketed strategies have popped up over the years, but the core elements we're covering in *Your Property Jumpstart* ™ are tried and tested, and have remained consistent winners over time.

Don't confuse yourself.

Stay focused, get liquid, build wealth.

BONUS CONTENT

Visit YourPropertyJumpstart.com/bonus
for your secret bonus chapter, the Protege Deal Calculator,
and additional content and resources to support you
on your property journey

CHAPTER 7:
RAISING FINANCE

We've come a long way.

We started with the Property Millionaire Mindset, discussing the importance of becoming the kind of person who can do the deals, as opposed to simply knowing the mechanics of them. We then moved into the foundations, fundamentals, jargon, your property power team, and understanding the groundwork and basic essentials of property. We then went into due diligence and Goldmine Areas, discussing the importance of having set criteria, and knowing your patch like the back of your hand. Then, we moved on to discuss buy-to-let, buy-to-flip, and deal packaging; going deep on the numbers.

Now, we're going to take this a step further, and get into various other essential elements of running a successful property business.

This chapter is one of my favourites, because it's all about the money.

Truth is, it doesn't matter how much money you have, even if you have £1m to start with. When you've invested that money the right way, with the investment strategies we've shown you, what do you do next? Well, you need to do the same thing that the person who started from zero is doing, and raise more funds.

There's always going to be deals. Trust me on that.

Your focus, aside from bringing the deals in, is being able to source the funds for your deals that allow you to keep on doing more and more. Your ability to do more deals depends entirely on your ability to raise finance. If you're anything like I was when I started in property in my late teens / early twenties, I had no money whatsoever. I had access to credit cards, loans, and overdrafts which I utilised not for property, but to fund my education. That education cost me tens of thousands of pounds, and you're getting a download of it in this book.

Many people have said to me that they don't have funds. "I don't have money to start. I'd love to get involved in property, but I don't have any money."

Well, here's what you need to ask yourself when it comes to raising finance...

WHY SHOULD ANYONE GIVE YOU ANY MONEY?

Who are you? More to the point, who are you in their eyes?
How have you positioned yourself? How do others see you?
Do you walk the talk? Do you know what you're talking about?
Why would anyone want to joint venture with you?
Do you have a track record?
Do you have knowledge that they don't?
Do you have the ability to go out and source deals?
Can you show them the type of deals you're sourcing, and the numbers?
Do you hold yourself well on social media?

These are the kind of questions you have to ask yourself. At the Property Protege ™ Intensive, we work on completely turning around your ability to become the kind of person worthy of raising finance, but understand this: right now, you can make a decision to change how you're seen, almost overnight. It's called social media. You're painting a picture to the world; make sure it's the right one.

When I started, we didn't have much in the way of social media, and I certainly wasn't credible in terms of track record or education, and it didn't help that I looked about 12 years old. However, my attitude was on point, I knew what I was talking about, I was able to source and identify the right deals, and I was aggressive in my approach. People could see that I was going somewhere, and they wanted whatever I had to offer.

RAISING FINANCE

WAYS TO RAISE FINANCE

Let's explore a handful of strategies to raise finance.

Again, we go deep on this and open the floodgates at Property Protege ™, but I want to arm you with a handful of powerful strategies here and now that, when applied, will make all the difference.

HOW'S YOUR CREDIT?

Let's start with the basics.

The first thing you should do is check your credit report. Fill in the essentials, and then find out your score. Is there any adverse credit or defaults on there that you didn't know about that you could potentially have removed? Is your information up-to-date and complete? I know that many people will have a poor credit rating; it's the way our country is wired for the most part, but if possible, make sure your credit report is tip-top, and work on improving it. You don't have to have good credit to succeed in property, not in the least, but at later dates, you may be exploring more substantial developments and you may need a half decent credit report in place to appease funders.

So what if you don't have a good credit score?

Well, that's when we begin to approach friends, family, colleagues, and others, as potential joint venture partners, or simply to invest in you and your deals.

LEVERAGING DEBT

Before we dig deeper on raising finance, we have to understand that debt can be a good thing, as opposed to public perception that debt is bad. That is, providing we utilise debt and put it towards creating a greater return.

Let's say you choose to utilise bank loans, credit cards, overdrafts, savings from ISAs, or equity from property. All of these ways of accessing funds will come with a cost for finance in the form of an annual percentage rate (APR). Let's say you were able to obtain a bank loan that gives you £10,000 with an APR of 50%. What you need to consider is that if you pay off the loan faster than the initial term, then you will actually pay less interest. The goal when leveraging debt is to pay it back as soon as possible, and then leverage again.

The mindset we want to adopt, is one of "How fast can I utilise these funds so I can pay back the debt plus interest, leaving me with profit left over to use for the next deal or to further leverage debt."

Having borrowed £10,000 with a 50% APR over 36 months, at the end of the 3 years you'd have paid back the initial £10,000 plus £9,481 in interest, with a total payback of £19,481. Now, this is an extreme example, as 50% APR is for those who have very bad credit and are deemed high risk. However, with this example I want to simply illustrate that it doesn't matter what the APR is, providing you put those funds to good use.

Let's say you invest the £10,000 that you borrowed into a buy-to-flip. You source the deal that meets your criteria, and choose to joint venture with someone, where both parties contribute towards the acquisition costs. Let's say you have structured the deal in a way that both of you are 50:50 partners. Let's say that the profit happens to be £20,000, giving you profit of £10,000. If you then added this to your original £10,000 and did another flip with the same investor on the same basis and the second deal also had a profit of £20,000, giving you another £10,000 each. Twelve months pass, and you have now turned that original £10,000 loan into £20,000 profit. Now that's a 200% return on your investment before you factor in the cost of finance from the loan. Now at this stage you could continue to leverage the £10,000 loan or decide that you want to pay off the loan early. Well, because you have paid the loan off early, the interest will only have been £2,910 with a total loan payback amounting to £12,910.

In this example, you started with no money at all, and leveraged debt through a high interest loan. You have made £20,000 and paid back £12,910 in total, leaving you with £7,090, which equates to a 70% return on your invested capital, including interest payments. To further simplify, you borrowed money at a 50% APR, and because you repaid the high interest loan in twelve months, you made 20% return on money that wasn't yours in the first place. If you have good credit, you will likely get an APR closer to 10%, or even lower, which means your return on leveraging debt will be much higher. You should apply this same mindset when leveraging all forms of borrowed money and debt.

I have yet to find a single person who became wealthy purely by saving money. You have to have your own, or borrowed, money out there working for you, providing the return is greater than the overall cost.

THE MINDSET OF RAISING FINANCE

There are many strategies available for raising finance; more than you might imagine, but none of them will work for you to their full capacity if you don't first work on your mindset around raising finance. Earlier in the book, we discussed your wealth thermostat. This is an area where your thermostat comes into play. The thought of going out to raise £100,000 may frighten people off, and the idea of asking for those funds terrifies them. My experience in working with thousands of people, is that we make a big deal about raising £25,000 to £50,000 for our first deal or two, when in reality, those are the easiest funds to secure.

Let's say you have secured a great deal, and all the numbers work for your investment criteria, but you don't have the acquisition costs to purchase the property. You may not even have good credit, so your ability to leverage a mortgage is out of the question at this stage. You already know that you could package the deal and trade to an investor for a fee, however, this deal ticks your own boxes to either add to your portfolio or flip, and you want to make it your *own* deal. My mindset has always been, "I would rather have 50% of something than 100% of nothing."

Believe it or not, but the financing of the deal and securing funds is the easiest part of the process, which we'll discuss. It's the sourcing of the deal, it's the structuring of the deal, it's securing the deal, that presents most challenges, and even those parts don't have to be difficult when you utilise the tools and resources we're providing you with to help you make it happen.

So let's say this deal is perfect for a flip, and after factoring in all acquisition costs and selling costs, you are set to make £15,000 profit. By applying the methods of raising finance that I'm about to cover, you could have a joint venture partner come in on the deal and front the acquisition costs for either a percentage return on their investment, or as a 50:50 partner splitting the profit.

Let's look at both options here; the first being a percentage return on their investment. Let's say the acquisition costs to purchase the property, the deposit, renovation costs, professional fees and all other associated costs comes to £30,000. Once the property is sold, there's profit of £15,000, and you've structured the deal with the investor / private funder that they receive a 15% return on their invested capital. £30,000 of the investors capital x 15% = £4,500. Of the £15,000 profit, you're left with £10,500.

Alternatively, if you chose to go in on the deal with a joint venture partner on a 50:50 profit share; you both would be set to make £7,500 each, equating to a 25% return on their initial investment. Keep in mind that you should be turning a buy-to-flip around inside six months, from the time of purchasing, to the time of selling, and if you were to take a joint venture partner into a second deal which was lined up for the next six month period, you'd be doubling the investor's return.

In the first example, the investor would make £4,500 on two property deals (based on the same type of deals and numbers), meaning their profit inside of twelve months would be £9,000, representing a 30% return on their invested capital over twelve months, while you have made £21,000 working with only one private investor on a percentage return basis, and having only secured two properties. With the second scenario, both you and your joint venture partner would receive £15,000 over the twelve month period, representing a 50% return on the joint venture partners investment.

These are two very simple and straight forward ways of structuring a joint venture. Where else are people going to find returns of 30%+ on their money? There are many ways to structure a joint venture, and the simpler the better. My experience has always been that once you give your joint venture partners strong returns, as above, you will have preferred investors for life. You can very quickly create a six-figure business working with only a handful of preferred investors who continually do deals with you, rather than continually having to sell to one-time investors who will not be long-term partners.

I hope that from this example you can start to see serious income coming into your property business, and that by simply doing a deal or two with one or two preferred investors, you will very quickly be able to replace your full-time income, becoming a full-time property investor or developer, if that is your goal.

THE RAISING FINANCE MYTH

There's a different game at play when it comes to financing property, and you can choose to play that game, or continue to operate how you always have done, with the same mindset that currently restricts people's ability to raise finance. Almost everyone's initial thought process around raising finance for their deals is focused on themselves; on their own ability to come up with funds, based on credit, savings, and so on. When it comes to raising finance, we must learn to get creative. We must think beyond our credit report and traditional methods of funding, particularly if your credit is poor and no high street bank will give you money. We must instead think beyond ourselves and look to unconventional means of raising funds. This is a big focus at Property Protege ™, as raising finance is the number one skill you must master. If you master the skill of raising finance you will go beyond a handful of deals, to literally having no limits to the number of deals you can be involved in, providing of course that your deals *are* deals.

Let's talk about one of the biggest myths to raising finance that holds people back from raising unlimited levels of finance. The biggest myth is that it's hard to raise finance and get the money. If we consider that statement to be true, or even entertain the thought, you will find that your subconscious mind begins to search for similar thoughts, past experiences, and reference points that back up the idea and make it true. It could be something as simple as a throwaway comment, but it comes back to reinforce the idea that raising finance is hard. What if we decided to adopt a different idea or affirmation around raising finance; that it was easy? What if we chose to change our language, our focus, and our attitudes towards raising funds, in a way that supports and reinforces our new perspective?

Here's my guarantee to you…

If you do a minimum of 2 financial presentations every week for 50 weeks, that's 100 financial presentations inside a year. My guarantee to you is that if you do this, you will raise the funds you've been looking for. If you want to accelerate the process, you might want to do 10 financial presentations each week for 10 weeks, which in turn will allow you to raise funds sooner.

Now let me clarify what I mean by a financial presentation…

A financial presentation is not a Powerpoint presentation or a spreadsheet full of numbers; it's simply the act of speaking with someone who could potentially be a joint venture partner, a private funder, a commercial lender, or quite simply anyone with the means of accessing funds to invest in you or your deals. This is your chance to share your vision, and equally to qualify them to see if they will be the right fit for you. This is not about begging for money; it's the opposite. There's so much money out there, that once you get good at doing financial presentations, you will have people queuing up to invest with you. Many of the people coming off the back of our Property Protege ™ Intensive weekends, find themselves raising funds that were right in front of their noses all along, only days after the event.

In order to make this a success, you must plan your financial presentation and make sure you tailor it to the individual you are going to meet rather than simply pitching the same old pitch over and over. You must review how your financial presentation went, asking yourself tough questions on why you didn't receive investment, if you didn't.. Did you ask for too much? Maybe not enough? Was the setting all wrong? Were you not prepared? Could you not adequately handle an objection?

Reviewing your financial presentations, allows you to learn from them and to improve for the next one. Plan the presentation ahead of time, rehearse, and think of questions you may be asked about you, your deals or your strategy. Think of the most common objections you'll receive and practice handling them. Present yourself well by the way you dress and where you meet the potential investor. Continue to review after each and every presentation you do, and ultimately, you will get the funds you're looking for. It may take you until presentation 10, or 20, or 50, but it will happen providing you continually improve and work towards the outcome you're looking for. My bet is, that it will be under 10 presentations if you truly apply this method as outlined.

PRIVATE FUNDING

One of the most exciting things about property, is that you generally shouldn't be using your own money. It's not a bad thing to do so, and it may be how you get your start, but leveraging other people's money is a timeless principle, and if we look back at the points we've discussed thus far in this chapter, we can relate each form of borrowing to that of the individual who is backing us.

Private funding can come from friends, family, work colleagues, business associates, and anyone who's prepared to invest in you or your deal for a fixed return. They know you're going to use the money to buy property, and they know that their money can be protected by taking a first charge over the property that you're about to go and buy, or if leveraging a mortgage, they would secure their interest through a solicitor. It might be a 50:50 partnership split, or it might be that they get a percentage on their funds, or whatever you and they are happy with.

We have investors who invest £100,000+ per annum for a 10% annual return. We leverage that money by applying the same principles we've covered so far, making it worth way more than 10% to us, giving the investors their return, with everything over and above that being profit for us and our business.

Why on earth would anyone give us £100,000 for just 10%? Wouldn't they want a bigger piece of the cake. Actually, not necessarily. A lot of people just want a hands-off approach to get a better return on their money. They have funds in the bank doing nothing, and they'd rather have it working for them, and are happy with a hands-free 10% return. They don't want to be involved in the hassle or hustle or issues; they just want the return. You're going to find lots of people like this, and the more of these people you find, the more and more deals you can do. Provide them with a return, and you'll find them back for more.

Here's another little note…

Sometimes, people in your life will simply give you funds to back you; investing in you personally. You could simplify this and simply call it borrowing.

EQUITY RELEASE

Equity release from your own home, or the property of someone privately funding you, is sometimes the cheapest and easiest option for borrowing. A lot of people are so focused on trying to pay down their own home mortgage, but they could be leveraging that money.

Whatever the equity you have in your home, you should speak with your Mortgage Broker to see what the best products available are, for you to access through releasing additional funds from the equity you or they have in the property.

Let's say you release £100,000 from your own or someone else's home. That's only going to be a few hundred pounds a month in interest that has to be covered each month, making it one of the cheapest forms of borrowing available as the interest is normally very low.

COMMERCIAL FUNDING

There are countless commercial lenders out there who are all fighting for your business, and they are becoming more and more competitive with their fees and interest rates. You have high street banks who offer commercial borrowing, to challenger banks who have less strict criteria as to what and who they'll lend to. Then there are smaller commercial lenders, to bridging finance.

Commercial finance is a form of bridging finance, however the reason I use both terms, is that bridgers tend to be smaller firms who either use their own personal funds or investor's funds, to provide short-term loans, and have their own set criteria as to what, and who, they will lend to. Normally, they will lend based on how strong the deal is, rather than focusing on the actual investor or purchaser of the deal. Commercial lenders who are underwritten by high street banks, or accountable to directors or shareholders, will have certain criteria that is set by the company, that the deal and investor must meet, before lending will be approved. The good news is there are many types of these lenders in the market right now. It's your job to go out there and meet as many of them as possible.

When meeting lenders, ask them what type of deals they invest in, and what their criteria is. What you'll find, with a number of commercial lenders, particularly bridgers, is that they will have different loan-to-value ratios compared to main stream lenders. This is normally much higher, with the average being 80% loan-to-value. This means you can increase your borrowings and have less of a deposit to put down. Commercial lending and bridging finance are the routes you'd want to pursue to purchase a property that is deemed uninhabitable or which needs substantial renovation works carried out, as most traditional high street lenders avoid lending on these types of properties.

As well as having a higher loan-to-value, if the deal is structured in the correct manner and there is substantial value to be added through renovation, the commercial lender or bridgers may increase their loan-to-value up to the end-value of the property.

An example of this would be if you purchased a property that required a full renovation with a current market value of £75,000. Let's say you bought the property at a very small discount of 10%; this would make the purchase price £67,500. Let's say you approached a number of commercial lenders and bridgers, finding out what they'd lend on, what their requirements were regarding the purchaser, and to discuss their finance terms. Let's say you have one lender who will give you a loan-to-value of 80% of the end-value of the property, as opposed to the current value of the property, and not the purchase price. Remember if you use traditional lenders, they will lend on the purchase price or valuation of the property, whichever is the lowest. This is not the case with most commercial lenders.

So let's say the end-value of the property after a full renovation to walk-in condition, is going to be £100,000. This would mean that the commercial lender or bridger would lend £80,000. That's enough to cover the purchase price of £67,500, as well as the renovation costs of let's say £10,000, with purchasing fees such as legal fees and stamp duty of let's say £3,500, giving you a total of £81,000. In this example, the commercial lender or bridger, would release £80,000, meaning you have all of the required funds, with only £1,000 to put into the deal. That's 100% finance in this example. Let's say the renovation happened to be £5,000 more, then in this case, you would only have to contribute £6,000 to the deal, which is substantially less than what you would normally need as acquisition costs to purchase the property.

The key takeaway here, is that if you find the right commercial lender or bridger, they will increase their funding limits if the deal stacks, and lenders are out there in abundance.

There are a few things that you should be aware of.

The first is that commercial finance costs are much higher than traditional lending, with higher interest rates, and in most of the cases have higher arrangement fees and exit fees with higher interest penalties if you go over the agreed time frame of the loan period. As you build a track record and do multiple deals with these companies, they will start to reduce their interest rates as well as reduce or remove their upfront and exit fees due to the repeat business and ease of working with a professional. In the beginning you may have to put up with factoring in the higher fees, just to get started. Bridging finance tends to attract higher interest rates, sometimes double or triple what you'd pay with commercial lenders, but are more flexible with lending terms. Bridgers also have options to roll-up the finance, meaning you don't pay any monthly interest payments until the end of the loan term, which is normally when you sell or refinance to a traditional, lower interest, lender.

You can always negotiate on both the commercial and bridging fees. Some are open to the discussion while others are very strict with their terms. The more of a track record you build and the more deals you do, the more favourable terms you'll receive.

Depending on the size of the renovation, particularly if it's in the tens of thousands, or even hundreds of thousands, the commercial lender or bridger will allow you to draw down on the development finance part of the funds. Meaning, that once you hit certain stages of the renovation and this is verified, they will release the next staged payment to continue with the renovation. You would only be paying interest payments on the funds, as and when you use them, at each stage of the renovation.

A lending product that many commercial lenders have, is a 'refurbish-to-let' product. In the same example as above, the lender would provide you with commercial funding at the higher rates to purchase and renovate the property. Let's say from the day you purchase the property you carry out the renovation inside four weeks. This meaning, having only owned the property for four weeks, you would contact the commercial lender, they would send out their valuer to revalue the property up to the new walk-in condition value. They would then allow you to refinance onto their own buy-to-let product with (in most cases) lower interest rates. This is the ideal product if you want to pull your funds out on a buy and hold strategy as fast as possible. Remember the six month guide that traditional lenders adhere to with regards to having to hold a property for a minimum of six months before you can sell or refinance? Well, due to you staying with the same lender, and with commercial lenders not adhering to the six month guideline, you can refinance inside the six months and pull your money out.

Many commercial funders and bridgers will want to see a track record. They'll want to see who your power team are. They'll want to know who your builder is. If you are just starting out and appear to have no track record, my suggestion would be to partner up with another investor or developer who does have a track record. By doing this, sure you'll be giving away a negotiable slice of the profit, but you'll have given yourself a massive advantage and began building your own track record.

Commercial and bridging lenders will lend to companies as well as individuals. The benefits of borrowing as a company is the flexibility, and depending on your own personal circumstances, you may have tax benefits too. It allows you to flip properties with your company, or hold properties as your company, meaning the business can start to build up an asset base, meaning you can always sell the business along with its assets as an exit in the future, which again, has tax benefits as well as leveraging power.

One thing to keep in mind, is that commercial and bridging lenders will look for as much security as possible. They would, in first instance, take a legal charge registered as a first charge against the property you are going to be purchasing and will not allow for any additional charges to be put against the title. They may also want to take some form of additional security in the form of a second charge over equity in your own home or additional properties you may own. Finally, they may ask for a personal guarantee; normally for the interest amount due to be repaid.

(Side Note: a legal charge is the means by which lenders enforce their rights to a property. There are different types of legal charge and the type used will vary from lender to lender. A primary mortgage will normally be secured by a registered first charge against the property while an additional mortgage or secured loan would be registered as a second charge)

SUMMARY

I hope you're beginning to realise that there's a whole new world of finance out there, and all we've covered here are a few select funding routines. At Property Protege ™, we share multiple strategies in depth, for raising finance way above and beyond what we've had the opportunity to share here. We break each strategy down, we role play, we practice financial presentations, we show people how to develop instant track records, we demonstrate and act out how to negotiate with commercial and bridging funders, and we dig deeper on more advanced methods of pulling in the funds.

That being said, what's been shared here has allowed some of our students to raise funds at the lower-end average of £20,000 to the higher-end £100,000+ in joint venture finance off the back of these simple strategies. Others, particularly those who attend Property Protege ™, find themselves armed with the knowledge, resources and confidence to release up to and beyond £1,000,000 in finance or funds towards their deals.

Raising finance is the master skill.

And it's never a question of resources; it's always a question of resourcefulness.

Let's keep this simple.

On the one hand we find the deals.

On the other hand, we find the money.

We then sit in the middle and manage.

That's business, that's entrepreneurship, that's property.

BONUS CONTENT

Visit YourPropertyJumpstart.com/bonus
for your secret bonus chapter, the Protege Deal Calculator,
and additional content and resources to support you
on your property journey

CHAPTER 8:
SUCCESSFUL JOINT VENTURES

A joint venture (JV) simply put, is two or more people working together for mutual benefit. This can be short-term or long-term. It could be one property transaction, many transactions, or being involved in a business together. There are many ways that joint ventures can be structured.

So why do it? Why joint venture?

There are many reasons you may want to joint venture. Perhaps you can't get a mortgage. Perhaps you don't have funds for a deposit. Perhaps you need help with certain aspects of your property business. Perhaps you need someone on-side with more experience. Perhaps you need sweat equity or someone with a complimentary skillset.

In the early days of my own property business, joint ventures didn't appeal to me. I wanted to go out and buy lots of property on my own. I wanted to build this thing myself. However, I very quickly realised that I could only get a couple of mortgages in my own name, not to mention starting with no funds. Remember, even if you start with a million pounds, once those funds are put to work, what do you do, do you just stop? No, if you're anything like me, you'll always have deals on the go. So I realised that I needed JV partners to come in on properties I was buying in order to provide the finance in order to purchase the properties.

It's better to have 50% of something, than 100% of nothing, and if you're in a position where something is lacking, then joint ventures could be the best way forward, as they were for me.

Even to this day, I still go in on joint ventures with people. Joint ventures don't necessarily mean that you're going to have other people in your business for the rest of your life, nor does it mean you're tied to them in your other ventures. A joint venture should be in place to manage a specific project or outcome.

THE BENEFITS AND THE RISKS

On the plus side, joint ventures can be great for a number of things.

Joint ventures can give you access to new markets and new networks. When I say new markets, I mean in terms of Goldmine Area. Your existing Goldmine Area will be in a certain location, and of course, you're the authority in that location. You're doing all of your marketing there, and you know the area like the back of your hand. Then, you form an agreement with a joint venture partner who has the same level of knowledge and experience in another area, expanding your reach. When I say new networks, we have to remember that your network is your net-worth, and by going in on deals with a new joint venture partner, you're going to meet new people, and be able to tap into the network of your partner.

Joint ventures can increase your capacity and the level of business you can handle. Two heads are better than one, as they say. So with this in mind, you'll have two minds working on your business, allowing you to do much more, and bring more into your business as a result of increased capacity.

In a joint venture, the risks and costs are generally shared. If you're about to go into a property transaction on your own, and you're covering the costs, then you personally carry the burden of risk going forward. However, when you joint venture with someone, if something were to happen down the line, you have someone there to help you carry the load. In some scenarios, your joint venture partner will provide, for example, the funds, while you provide the sweat equity. In a situation such as this, you'd both generally share the burden of cost on maintenance and repairs.

In a joint venture, you may be working with someone who has a team behind them. That team, can then be leaned upon to support you in your efforts on the joint venture, bringing their knowledge and experience to the table, as well as providing a backbone to your business.

Of course, while there are pros, there are also various things to consider…

Joint ventures take time and effort in order to build strong relationships, and like any relationship, problems will arise. Many people entering joint ventures go in with no clear objectives, meaning no one has a set outcome or series of outcomes upon which to base the JV. It's imperative that outcomes are clearly defined from the beginning. Sometimes, if you choose to ignore outcomes and objectives, a breakdown in communication can occur, which can spell the end of a joint venture. Communication is key. It is vitally important. You must be able to speak openly and honestly; particularly when issues raise their head. The last thing you'd want to do, is let something fester in the back of your mind, only to come back to light at a later date.

It sounds obvious, but both joint venture partners must be clear on which strategies to employ. One person may want to focus on flips, while the other wants to focus on buy-to-let. Get it clear now, in order to avoid potential upset later.

Another problem I often see is an imbalance in anything from levels of expertise to who brought the money to the table. The question is, who's bringing what? You must be aware of the potential for imbalance to cause problems. Both partners will likely bring different skills, abilities and resources, and providing everyone is clear on the outcomes, on communication, on the time and effort that'll be put in, and the process is managed properly, you could have a great relationship in the making.

The final potential conflict for now, is differing opinions when it comes to management styles. You may have an entirely different management style from your joint venture partner, and if you're running teams or dealing with trades and so on, it's important to be clear with one another, and not to bang heads. It's likely that your joint venture partner will have strong opinions, after all, we entrepreneurs tend to know our own minds, but when you bang heads over how to deal with staff, or anything else for that matter, it stalls progress. Both you and your JV partner must sell the vision to the team, in order for the team to get behind it. Sometimes your JV partner will be the arrowhead and lead the charge in one area, whilst you focus on being the arrowhead and leading the charge in another.

PLANNING YOUR JOINT VENTURE RELATIONSHIP

When entering a joint venture relationship, the first thing you'll want to establish, is what each person is bringing to the table. This could be finances, assets, skillset, knowledge, time, or sweat equity. It could be absolutely anything. Don't overcomplicate this. Remember, a joint venture is simply two or more people working for mutual benefit. Your goal at the beginning, is to have a good discussion, establish each person's contribution, write down the parts that each of you are going to play, and ensure that each person understands the outcomes of working together; what you're looking to achieve. When you've established the outcome or objection, break it down, create the plan, and be clear on what has to happen next.

It's important to have realistic expectations in a joint venture. Now, I'm all for thinking big, but I'm also realistic in terms of what can be achieved when it comes to a joint venture. When you work with someone for the first time, don't get caught up in chat about taking over the world or buying hundreds of properties. Focus on the task at hand, and if that realistic outcome moves forward, then move focus to the next, and let the relationship unfold and build upon success.

Is there trust between partners? The objectives you agree upon will turn into what you'd call a working relationship, where trust is essential, and each person is doing what they said they would, minus the need to check up on each other. Talk openly with your partner and ensure that there is clarity around roles and responsibilities, and then carry out your part with full effectiveness. If you do not trust your partner, or your partner does not trust you, then the relationship will not work.

CHOOSING YOUR JOINT VENTURE PARTNER

So we've established the benefits of a joint venture partnership, as well as the upside and the risks, and we've also discussed the planning phase. So how do you choose a joint venture partner in the first place? Here are a few things to think about when selecting JV partners...

We've discussed the importance of establishing who's bringing what to the table. That's natural when it comes to joint ventures. What should also be considered when entering an agreement, is the resources and skills of others that compliment your own. We all have our unique abilities, talents, contacts, and so on. When we partner up with people who have the same skills, the same talents and the same network, it doesn't allow for much potential in expansion. Joint ventures aren't about finding someone who's identical to you. It's about finding someone who brings aspects to your business that you don't have, whether skills, finances, or resources; whatever it's going to be.

It's important that your joint venture partner is like-minded. You don't need to love the person, or even like them, but you do have to be like-minded. You have to be able to get on with them and do business with them. You must also share the same desired outcomes and end results.

Before you start signing agreements, you may want to test them. If they say that they're bringing work ethic to the table, why not find a scenario where you can establish exactly how reliable their work ethic is? If they say they're always ready for action, why not arrange a meeting at a difficult time of day. If they can't show up when things are easy going, it's quite possible that they won't measure up when things get tough and you need them to be there. What's their attitude to partnerships? Do they think only of themselves, or are they team players? Are they covering themselves, or are they out to secure both of your interests? Can you trust them? If there's any element of doubt in the trust category, kill the deal immediately. When little things start to creep in, if there's no trust, it'll only grow and create much bigger problems down the line. What kind of reputation do they have? Don't be afraid to speak to other people and ask them about the person you're about to go into business with. See if they're seen in a positive light, or if others have had negative experiences with them, and weigh it all up.

You may want to take your JV due diligence a step further and find out whether they are financially secure. If they're not financially secure, that doesn't necessarily mean you shouldn't go into business with them; it just means that you're going in with your eyes wide open. For example, if someone is struggling financially, it's only a matter of time before they need to start taking income from the business, which is another reason why all outcomes and finer points must be established from the word go. Do they have credit problems? This may be something that comes into play if you're applying for joint finance, or even in something as simple as opening a joint bank account. Do they have other business interests? Depending on the intensity and scope of what you'll be doing together, it's important to know how much of them you can expect. If they have other interests, it's not a good or bad thing, it's just something to be aware of going in. Do they have a track record? Again, if they don't, that's not the end of the world, but it's good to know.

I've said it before and I'll say it again: everyone must know their roles. Whether full-on or passive, sweat equity or financial, backseat or arrowhead, we must know where we fit. With this established, you can then measure performance through regular communication. Everything I'm sharing here comes from things I learned the hard way. For example, I remember one particular joint venture in the early days, where I was pushing, grafting, hustling and stressing, whereas my partner wouldn't even pick up the phone because he was taking days off, heading to the sauna, relaxing on long weekends away. Before long, resentment kicked in, followed by a breakdown in communication, and before I knew it, we'd went our separate ways. It was messy. I don't want the same thing to happen to you. With this said, make sure you put each part of what's being discussed here into play, and make sure that as well as establishing outcomes and measuring performance, there's also an element of flexibility, for the very reason that this needs to be open and fun, as well as subject to life's curveballs.

Finally, when selecting your joint venture partner, if it hasn't already been blatantly obvious, communication is going to be essential. Whether face-to-face, or regular audio notes or phone calls, it's important to have regular chats with your joint venture partners. If the arrangement is more passive and longer term in nature, your communication won't be as frequent, but if a project is a little more intensive, you'll want to stay in regular contact and keep the loop open. When communicating with your JV partner, it's important to share and talk openly. The last thing you want is to say something and find your joint venture partner doesn't know about it because you haven't been open about things, particularly when it comes to financial matters such as what's in the bank, what's been spent, and so on.

SECURING YOUR INTERESTS

Once we've established the fit and selected a partner we feel we can work with, we must recognise the importance of documenting our interests. This basically starts as a blank piece of paper, where both parties write down and agree upon the terms and conditions of the agreement, the structure of the joint venture, the objectives of the joint venture, and any little caveats or clauses. This can then become a signed and legal document with the help of your solicitor. This shouldn't be an uncomfortable exercise; it's simply an understanding between both parties, which will prevent any misunderstandings.

What's the management control of certain parts of the business in terms of the roles each person will assume? What responsibilities must be taken care of by each person? How are liabilities, profits and losses shared? Is the burden on one person or is it down the middle? How will disputes be resolved if they arise? Through a third-party mediator, or a solicitor? What does the exit strategy look like? Are you focusing on buy-to-let, or buy-to-flip, or a bit of both? Are you in for one deal, or multiple deals? Are you tied to the person or not? If a relationship blossoms, then all of this can be changed, but start strong, for the benefit of both parties.

Joint ventures can be powerful. We're all human, and we all have our limits in terms of capital, resources, time, sweat equity, and so on. Leveraging the resources of others for mutual benefit, can be a fantastic vehicle. Make sure, as we've discussed, that you've gone in with your eyes wide open, that you know your outcomes, that you've done your homework and selected someone that'll be the perfect fit, and make sure, for both of your benefit, that you've tied it all up in legal documentation.

So, we've come a long way.

We've covered the Property Millionaire Mindset. We've covered the foundations and fundamentals. We've covered due diligence and mastering our Goldmine Area. We've covered various long-term and short-term investment strategies. We covered raising finance. Finally, we've covered joint ventures, allowing you to go in with other people to further expand your property ambitions and make big things happen. We've covered a lot, but we're not done yet.

Let's talk about how we find the deals…

BONUS CONTENT

Visit YourPropertyJumpstart.com/bonus
for your secret bonus chapter, the Protege Deal Calculator,
and additional content and resources to support you
on your property journey

CHAPTER 9:
PROPERTY DEAL SOURCING

So here's the thing...

We know what to do when we've sourced the deal.

So where do we find the deals in the first place?

If you can't find the deals, then you don't have a business.

Most people, let's call them amateurs, spend most of their sourcing efforts on building relationships with estate agents, and hunting RightMove, and while there are deals to be found on both fronts, it's a very populated space. Don't be surprised if you find yourself tripping over other local investors and sourcers while you're out on your travels, and don't expect to walk into an estate agent's office and have them say, "Awesome! There are no other investors I deal with. You're the first one, and I'm going to send all of the best deals to you, even though I don't know you."

It's not going to happen. Relationships take time, and agents already have their preferred investors. You should definitely do it, but with one or two agents rather than attempting to get to know all of them. Similarly with RightMove, you'll find other investors actively hunting for deals online, albeit you'll know more than they do because you've mastered your Goldmine Area, you know what walk-in condition looks like, you know where you can add value or more space, and you ultimately know a deal when you see one. But again, it's a populated space.

On the other side, professional investors are sourcing their own deals. They're marketing to local home owners and positioning themselves as the go-to guy (or girl) in their area. It may be surprising to hear that you should be looking for substantial discounts on properties, and you may be wondering why on earth anyone would want to take less money than what their property is worth, so let's discuss this...

First, we need to understand that deals are everywhere. The key words to keep in mind, are 'motivated sellers'. Think about it: motivated, sellers. If they're motivated, and they need to sell, then we can help them. And if they're motivated (are you getting this yet?) then you'll be in a position to make them an offer for a quick sale, which benefits them as they need to sell, and benefits you as the investor by securing a substantial discount.

So where do we find these people?

They're everywhere.

They're your friends, your family, your neighbours, and your colleagues.

Think about this. Do you know anyone who's in financial difficulty? Do you know anyone who's ever split from marriage or a long-term relationship? Do you know anyone who's died? Do you know anyone who's left the country to start a new life elsewhere? Do you know anyone who's downsized because the children have flown the nest? Do you know anyone who's been selling a property and buying another, and the person buying their property pulled out, leaving them unable to purchase their dream home?

We're talking normal people, from all walks of life, who are in situations where they need to sell, and don't have the luxury of time to sell on the open market. In many cases, it's not even financially motivated, and in many cases, the house is no longer their home, it's a burden, and something they need to sell fast in order to move forward. Some people may perceive this as taking advantage, but when a seller hugs you and thanks you profusely for stepping into the situation that they found themselves in, and helping them out of it, then you know you're doing a good thing.

So how do we find these motivated sellers?

First and foremost, if you make it known that you are in property, and you scrub up your image and become the kind of person who people want to deal with, you'll find many people getting in touch through the grapevine, through family and friends, or through social media.

The strategy we want to adopt aggressively, however, is to cast a wide net in a small area. We've discussed your Goldmine Area. Now, we want to dominate that patch. We want to be seen everywhere and anywhere. When someone walks into the local pub, or the bookies, or the post office, or the takeaway, or the vets, or the local shop, or when they stop their car at traffic lights, or pop into their local citizens advice bureau; we want to be there in our marketing. Everywhere, anywhere, all the time. We want to be so well known and recognised, that people can't help but take notice. The great thing is, there are countless opportunities available to you to get in front of your ideal prospects, which we'll talk about here.

Above and beyond positioning yourself as the local go-to guy or girl, there's additional leverage in the form of positioning yourself as both "local" and the "expert." Let's face it, very few people want to deal with large multinationals on a very personal matter. Very few people want to call a number only to be met with another person who doesn't know them or their situation. Local solutions, and more to the point, experts in their fields, are becoming increasingly more dominant in providing solutions; be they financial or otherwise. Isn't it a great thing that 'little Mary' gets to sell her house to someone 'just down the road', who she can pick up the phone and talk to, and who actively wants to help her?

THE MARKETING

So let's talk about marketing.

Let's talk about how we reach our target market.

There's something you should know, however…

You are a marketer first, and everything else thereafter.

Small business owners are ultimately marketers first, before anything else. You may think of yourself as a trader, or an investor, or a property professional, but the fact is, before all of that, you are a marketer of solutions to people who need to sell their house fast, just as you are a marketer of solutions to people who want to invest in property or put their money to good use. You are a marketer first, and that's that. A good split I'd recommend, is to look at three areas of business: production, operations, and marketing. 20% of your time should be spent on production (or fulfilment), 20% of your time should be spent on systems and operations, and 60% of your time should be spent actively sourcing deals and raising finance; being the marketer. If you don't have deals or funds, then you do not have any need for the other two.

Before we discuss some specific essentials around marketing, there's one core element that must be in place. Ultimately, the backbone of what you do. This central point of all of your marketing efforts is a strong property sourcing website. Think about it. If you were making a buying or selling decision on something even smaller and less substantial than a property, and the company you were dealing with didn't have an online presence, how would you feel about them? Would you trust them? Would you find it difficult to establish their level of credibility? Would you look for an alternative solution? Your website is the central point of your efforts, because every piece of marketing you put out will have your website on it. Sure it'll also have your contact number, but it's significantly easier to remember a website address than a number, and more people would rather look for further information than pick up the phone.

With regards to securing a phone number, avoid mobiles, as it screams one-man-band. Avoid 0800 as it screams faceless corporation. Instead, visit a website such as TelecomsWorld, and rent a local number for a very low monthly fee. On websites such as TelecomsWorld and others, you can pay an average of £10 per month to rent a number that's local, and you then simply log in to your online dashboard, and pop your mobile number in, so that when someone calls the local number, they're put straight through to your mobile.

As for securing a website, it's vital that you get this right. You need a strong website targeting your Goldmine Area, positioning you as the local expert, establishing credibility, and one that's well made, well written, mobile and tablet friendly, and fast loading. Your website should have one outcome: establish credibility in order to have them fill in your short contact form; ultimately turning a visitor into a prospect.

To secure your website, visit **propertysourcingsolutions.com**

I personally own this company and our team have been trained based on what's been proven to work, through the efforts of our clients, and over my own 13 years being heavily involved in the sourcing of property deals. You can work with other companies, sure, but we know what works and how the game is played. To tap into that knowledge and take the fast-track to results, head to the website now.

Let's step back for a moment...

We know that you are a marketer first.

We know that big discounts are possible.

We know that we must position ourselves as the local expert.

We know where to get a contact number, and where to get our vitally important website.

But before we get into specific strategies, it's even more important to understand some basic marketing essentials. By understanding what follows, you'll be able to conduct the orchestra and manage each moving part. Remember, graphic designers aren't marketers, website designers aren't marketers, the people you'll instruct to create your materials, aren't marketers. If they were marketers, they wouldn't be doing your bidding, they'd be out there creating business for themselves. So if they're not marketers, then it's vital that you have that core, base-level understanding in order to understand the basics and oversee the work.

Here are some things to keep in mind...

We must test and measure. Every location is different. Every area has its own little mini-economy. What works well in one area, may not work as well in another. We must test, by going in and doing what we do, and then measure the response. We must always be measuring how well our marketing is doing, how well we convert, how many people come in through each source of marketing, and how much we've spent versus how much we've made. It's essential. By getting in the game, keeping your costs minimal, and finding out what's working and what's not, you can either cancel a specific strategy, adjust it to see if performance improves, or radically and aggressively increase what you're doing. To add to this, before we cancel or adjust anything, we must give it time to find its feet. Rarely will you be able to know what's working overnight. It takes time. Be patient and follow what you're learning here. Finally, make sure that every time someone comes through to you, the first thing you ask is, "So how did you find out about us? What made you get in touch?" and then document and track the results of your campaigns.

We must operate with common sense. Let's say you're sourcing properties in a housing estate on the south side of Glasgow. Would you have leaflets with pictures of green fields and a large country house on it? No, because you're not sourcing country mansions are you? A designer will use a template that looks good, but you have to see past it. On a similar note, make sure there's congruency in your marketing efforts. Don't have a purple business card, a minimalist white website, and a multi-coloured leaflet. Keep consistency in your branding, as it's going to start to stick in people's minds.

Your marketing content must be well written, using what's known in marketing chat as strong copy. The word 'copy' is short for copywriting, and doesn't refer to protecting intellectual property, rather, it refers to writing words that influence and sell. If you ever hear a marketer talk about the copy, they're referring to the words that ultimately influence and convert their readers. So, with this in mind, we must ensure that our leaflets, bandit boards, websites, and so on, are written with strong ad copy. I'll give you two ways to remember how to create strong copy, but if you head to propertysourcingsolutions.com you'll find pre-made leaflet templates, website solutions and more, to save you the hassle of overthinking this.

The first thing to remember when it comes to copy, is AIDA.

Attention, Interest, Desire, Action.

First, grab their attention. Second, hold their interest. Third, build their desire. And fourth, the 'call to action', meaning, tell them what to do next. Let's look at this in the form of a leaflet. The design of the leaflet and a strong headline such as 'SELL YOUR HOUSE FAST' will get their attention. The bullet points that follow will build their interest, and begin to turn it into desire. The instruction that follows, for example, "For a guaranteed offer on your property, visit XYZ Property Solutions" comprises desire and action.

The second thing to remember when it comes to copy, is WIFM.

What's in it for me?

You should always think in terms of what I like to call the 'So what?' test. In other words, why should anyone take notice of you, of your materials, of your services? Why should anyone read your leaflet? Why should anyone go through your website? What's in it for them? Too many companies focus on features over benefits. They detail irrelevant facts. Irrelevant, because it doesn't tell the prospect what's in it for them. In all cases, focus on what you can do for them in your marketing, and in how what you have to offer, is of benefit, to them.

MARKETING STRATEGIES

So now that we've covered the basic marketing essentials, let's talk about what you can actually do in your marketing efforts, and how you're going to reach people, powered by what we've already discussed.

So here's the thing…

From the moment we wake up in the morning, we're being marketed to.

Let's take an average guy or girl…

They wake up and check their phone. Whether on social media or email or both, they're being marketed to. They get up, turn on the radio or TV, and they're being marketed to. They get the morning paper, and you guessed it, they're being aggressively marketed to, including several leaflets falling out of the middle pages. They walk to the front door and there's mail, including various pieces of marketing. They head to the car to go to work. The radio comes on, they're being marketed to. They drive past billboards, into the petrol station for fuel, and every step of the way, from the big images to the petrol pumps to the countless magazines, promotions, newspapers, ad screens and offers, they're being marketed to. They've been up for an hour, and have barely gotten started on their journey, and they're being marketed to.

This is how it works. Every day, we see between 4,000 and 5,000 advertisements. That's 4,000 to 5,000 times each day we're being marketed to.

What's the point?

Well, if there are so many ways and means of other people marketing to you, then when you assume the role as the marketer, you have countless and endless resources available to you to market to others.

You become the producer, not the consumer.

As the marketer, you could take advantage of leaflets, postcards, bandit boards, print media, radio, direct mail, referrals, alliances, affiliation, networking, door knocking, ad screens, vehicle wraps, pay per click, Facebook ads, RightMove, billboards, and so on.

Which works best?

Remember, test and measure. We'd be here all day to go through each and every strategy, but if we approach each one with the marketing fundamentals we've discussed as the foundations and backbone, and we test and measure, we'll do pretty well.

Everywhere, anywhere, within your Goldmine Area, at all times.

IF I WAS TO START AGAIN TODAY

If I was to start from scratch in a new country, following the principles we've discussed here, let me tell you what my approach would be...

I'd start by having leaflets designed and printed. Low cost, but a time served and very powerful strategy. I'd hire a local company to distribute the leaflets on solo drops (as opposed to delivering along with other mail), or I'd pay a younger friend or family member to distribute on my behalf. I'd have my leaflets delivered to every home in my goldmine area, with the exception of homes that I know without doubt are local authority or council owned. I'd have them delivered every two to three weeks, on an ongoing and never-ending basis. The leaflets would be A5, and would be created following the marketing principles already discussed, or as found at propertysourcingsolutions.com. Leaflets may produce immediate returns, or, they may simply act to serve as positioning you as credible and consistent, whilst time plays its role in having people get in touch. People who find themselves in difficult circumstances tend to keep their head in the sand until the last possible minute. At this point, they become motivated, and even if you've been marketing to them for five months, it becomes worthwhile when they decide it's time to take action. The worst thing you can do with leaflets is to stop. You lose all momentum, and for the low cost involved, you will miss out on deals worth thousands upon thousands of pounds.

As well as leaflets going through doors, I'd ensure that either a postcard sized variation of the leaflet, or the larger sized leaflet itself, was placed in every pub, club, takeaway, restaurant, shop, bookies, public toilet, doctors waiting area, dentist waiting area, and citizens advice waiting area. Everywhere, and anywhere.

I'd have bandit board designs created at propertysourcingsolutions.com and printed on correx boards, similar in material and size to estate agency boards. I'd then have those boards positioned all around town. This can backfire if relevant permissions are not obtained, but with that in mind, why wouldn't you want to use proper means to have your advertisement positioned on a billboard or somewhere prominent. Remember, all places at all times. Bandit boards are at your own risk and have proved an extremely powerful and high converting strategy among our students at Property Protege ™.

As well as doing the above, which are all reasonably low cost, I'd begin to network with people at local networking events, meeting local accountants, advisors, solicitors, and anyone within the reach of my target customers, with whom I could build a relationship, leading to increased business, their way and my way.

On the online front, I'd ensure that I had my website in place, to have all traffic driven there. I wouldn't attempt to cheap out on my website, as I know that the quality will determine the results and paint a picture of my business. My website would establish credibility, would answer their questions in advance, and would be strongly written to have people fill in the offer form, allowing me to get in touch with them. I'd likely attempt to have my target location in the website domain name, for example CORONATION STREET HOME BUYERS, but I'd settle for another variation, so as long as the words 'home buyers' or 'house buyers' or 'property buyers' or similar were present. The team at propertysourcingsolutions.com will walk you through this. I've referenced this resource several times and with good cause. Everything you need is ready and waiting for you, cutting out the need for copywriting, design, creativity, testing, and so on.

I'd also want to take other steps on the online front, utilising Facebook's ad platform to target local home owners, and if I had funds available at the time, I'd be using Googles pay per click platform to go laser focused on people actively looking to sell their home in my area. Online ads can become very costly, but the question is, if you're doing it right, then is the return worth the investment? What are you willing to spend, in order to acquire a client? You don't get clients, you acquire them. This is the marketer's mindset.

A final note on the online front for now, is RightMove. By creating an account on RightMove, you can draw your target area on a map, and subscribe for email notifications every time a new property is added in your area. You can study RightMove daily to get a grip on local properties, local values, both those in need of work, and those in walk-in condition. If you truly grasp your local market, you'll be able to spot opportunities that other people miss, and you'll be able to move on them fast.

As we've said, there are countless ways and means of getting in front of people. The golden rule is: everywhere, anywhere, all of the time, inside your target area. If you follow the approach I would take if I was starting afresh, you'll have no problems sourcing deals.

After a while of marketing, you'll start to find people get in touch with you simply because they've heard of you. As you start to do deals, word of mouth will become your ally. There comes a point when you could even scale back on your marketing if you wanted, because business will continually walk in the door, but why would you want to cut back on a good thing.

The truth is, while all of this is easy to do, it's also easy not to do. Most people will read these words, be inspired by them, but choose not to push forward. Awesome; all the more for you. There is no competition for those who choose to take their position as a marketer first, and to be aggressive in their approach.

BONUS CONTENT

Visit YourPropertyJumpstart.com/bonus
for your secret bonus chapter, the Protege Deal Calculator,
and additional content and resources to support you
on your property journey

CHAPTER 10:
NEGOTIATION AND MAKING OFFERS

So now that we know how to source the deals...

We now need to bridge the gap between finding a motivated seller and creating a win-win outcome where they get to sell their property, and you get a deal that works for you.

This is where we must learn to negotiate.

Now, don't be scared by this word. The idea of negotiation can often be confused with high-pressured sales or underhand tactics. That's not what this is. Negotiation is simply the process of opening a dialogue where you go back and forth until both parties can walk away with a suitable outcome. When sourcing deals, and even when attending viewings where an agent isn't present, you'll become the negotiator.

DEALING WITH MOTIVATED SELLERS

Throughout the book, particularly in the sourcing section in the previous chapter, we've discussed the idea of sellers being motivated. The key word, as we've explained is 'motivated'. There has to be motivation behind their reason for the sale, and it's your job to find out what that is. Many amateur investors get caught up trying to negotiate big discounts without finding out more about the seller and their circumstances, and subsequently, yet not surprisingly, end up losing them.

Sellers want the ideal scenario. They want full market value and their property sold yesterday.

The reality is, we know that's not going to happen, so we need to listen to them, ask them quality questions, and work out a solution that's going to be right for them, and for us. We know our criteria, and we know our unbreakable investment criteria, so we're going to have to discuss the discount in order to know which potential exit strategy the property will fit, will it be one you'll add to your portfolio, or a flip, or a deal you'll package and sell to an investor.

Once you've done your initial fact find you need to explain to the seller what investors are looking for these days, and in return for getting a property sold quickly, assuming you're going down the packaging route, or considering it as an option, there's going to have to be a bit of come and go in terms of price. Let them know you can get the property sold quickly for them if the numbers work for the investors who'll be buying it. Again, this isn't high pressure chat, it's a discussion, laying out the facts and options.

You must manage the seller's expectations throughout the process. Let them know that if they want their property sold tomorrow then they are going to have to sell their property below market value, and they're going to have to take a hit on the sale price. If the seller had the luxury of an estate agent on the open market then chances are they're going to get a much better offer, but a truly motivated seller doesn't have the luxury to put their property on the market with an agent. They don't have the time because they have to sell now. So, you must manage their expectations and explain what an investor is going to expect in return for buying their property quickly.

You must be honest with the seller. Be yourself. Don't say things you can't back up, and don't make promises you can't keep. You're there to help them, and you're looking to provide a prompt, professional and courteous service throughout the process. If you go in with this attitude, you're going to find a solution that works for you and works for them. Whether you're dealing with a motivated seller over the phone initially, or in person, be honest and truthful. People can smell bullshit a mile away.

Motivated sellers are in a situation where they're vulnerable, so you need to be confident and assure them that you can deliver. Once you've gone through your questions and you've identified the information that's going to help you work out what offer you're going to submit, you need to go to them with the offer, and the solution that's going to help them. Speak to them with confidence that you can do what you've said you'll do. This confidence, is what's going to keep the seller feeling ok, knowing that they're dealing with a professional and that they have no reason to doubt you.

Throughout this process, sellers need support. They essentially need you to hold their hand throughout the process. From the first phone call or the first meeting, you need to hold their hand throughout the journey, keeping the communication open and letting them know of any issues that arise. Remember, they may be about to lose their home, depending on the situation they're in, and they need you to be there to be sincere with them, listen to them, and answer any questions they may have with confidence to help reassure them.

From the moment you first speak with a seller, let's say over the phone, you have to build a strong and lasting first impression. You have to bring that confidence, positive energy, an upbeat manner, and good rapport to the table. When you meet them in person, this must continue, and you must be conscious of how you dress, how you look, and how you present yourself. In terms of first impressions, are you taking the time to listen, to connect, and to show them that you understand their situation? Or are you jumping in too heavy. One of the most important principles of negotiation, is to listen first. People are always too eager to talk, but if we listen instead, we get more and more information, and the more we know, the better equipped we are to help. Building rapport and finding common ground, whether it be hobbies or your favourite football team, a motivated seller is going to connect with you if you're real, and once comfortable with you, then they're going to open up.

QUESTIONS ARE THE ANSWER

As we've discussed, the key is to ask questions and then listen, assessing their situation in order to find a solution that works for both parties. So let's talk about some of the questions you're going to want to ask. Again, this can be done over the phone or it can be done in person.

First and foremost, most people will contact you via your website, and in that process they'll be asked for their name, contact number, the address of the property, the property type, and number of bedrooms. You'll then have some basic information upfront to begin your due diligence. If the person calls you, or the lead does not come via your website, this is information you're going to have to ask for. The more information you get up front, the better, but what you don't want to do is ask for too much at the initial stage of opening the door to them, and potentially put them off.

Assuming you have their basic information, when you get to the phone call or meeting stage, you're going to want to know the answers to the following questions. I'd recommend getting what you need on the phone and if the situation feels right, get along to view the property.

What's the current condition of the property?

It's vital to know the true condition of the property so that you're aware of what work may be required to bring it up to walk-in condition. If you know your Goldmine Area and the property values for the area, then you'll be able to work out the current value of the property. The seller may say it's in good condition, but then you find out that the reality is it needs a new kitchen and bathroom. Well, you'd then have to account for the cost of a new bathroom and new kitchen. Does the property have gas central heating? Does it have double glazing? This kind of thing is important, so don't be afraid to ask. On the flip side, have they had extra work done to the property? For example, an extension, or loft conversion, or new windows.

Having as much information as possible will help you formulate a picture of the property in its current condition in order to get an indication of what the value is going to be. You need to factor this information in so that you're able to determine what you're going to offer.

Why are they selling the property?

Why are they selling in the first place? A lot of people forget to ask this basic question, but this is where the motivation lives. This is about finding out exactly what their reasons are for selling, and if you can get past the surface level chat to the bottom of the issue, you'll be better able to help them, and better able to negotiate, knowing and understanding their driving force.

Some people will be facing repossession. Some people will be in financial difficulty. Some people will be relocating and struggling to sell their current property. Some people will be emigrating and struggling to sell. Some people will be facing divorce and their property will have become a burden. Some people will find themselves left with inherited properties they don't want. Some people will be part of a chain that's been broken, and find themselves unable to move forward because the buyer of their property pulled out of the purchase. Some people will be amateur landlords who panic at the first sign of change and who want out of property.

There are many reasons why someone will sell, and why they'll be motivated.

It's up to you to find out, and to gauge their level of motivation.

How quickly do you want to sell?

If someone needs to sell tomorrow, then you're going to have to make an offer that has a big enough discount to get investors interested. If the seller has more time to wait, then the discount doesn't have to be as high because you have more time to find investors. Keep in mind that if they can't take the big discount, a quick sale price so to speak, then you'll have to explain to them that it'll take you longer to find an investor. Investors are looking for bigger discounts, generally 25% below market value or more, and if they can't accept an offer at that sort of price, then they're going to have very few investors interested.

How much is the outstanding mortgage?

You'll need to know what the outstanding mortgage amount is, if they have any secured loans, or if they are in arrears. These things are vitally important to know, as is every other piece of information we're gathering, because when you make an offer you need to make sure that your offer will pay off the mortgage, associated loans, and the arrears. If you don't get this information up front, you could be about to go ahead with the purchase, and your solicitor finds out that the mortgage is much higher than your offer, which will make you look like an amateur, waste everyone's time, and present an issue with the offer.

When is a good time to visit the property?

If you're dealing with a seller over the phone, you need to ask them when you can visit the property. It's important for you to see the property to get a true understanding of its condition, but more importantly, you'll want to meet the seller in person in order to introduce yourself, establish rapport, and help them work on the situation. The phone is a starting point, but providing you get a pulse on the situation and know that it could potentially be a deal, you'll want to get that in-person meeting set up ASAP.

Further to the questions we've just gone through, you may want to ask if the property is currently being marketed by an estate agent, and if so, how long it has been on the market. If the property has been on the market for some time, then they will likely be open to a quicker sale and reduce the asking price to get it. You may want to ask what they think the estimated value of the property is. Of course many sellers will state a figure that's much higher than the actual value, but this then gives you the opportunity to manage their expectations. In some cases they'll say a lot less, so you can use this as a starting point when it comes to your negotiation and in what you're going to offer. If the seller has an estimated value in mind, you have to ask where they came up with the number. Was it from a surveyor who valued the property? If so, was it recently, or several years ago? Did their friend tell them what it would be worth based on their knowledge of another local sale? Again, it's important to gain as much information as possible, in order to manage their expectations, and establish the base upon which to make your offer.

NEGOTIATING WITH SELLERS

In the early days, before I had teams going out and handling the negotiations for me, I did all of the negotiation myself. I would follow up with each and every lead that we'd sourced through our marketing efforts, spending hundreds upon hundreds of hours negotiating with sellers, both on the phone, and in person. As a result, I began to formulate my own rules around negotiation. You wouldn't want to go into a scenario where you robotically stick to everything I say here. Rather, you'd want to develop your own little armoury, and make negotiation second nature, including the principles we're discussing here. Fluidity is vital. The ability to have a conversation, and naturally influence another person, is where it's at.

The first thing you'll want to do, is know your limit on what you're prepared to offer to make that deal work for the exit strategy you're banking on. Whether that's adding to your portfolio, doing a flip, joint venturing, or if you are going to package up and sell onto an investor. You have to know your limit in order for it to work. That doesn't mean that knowing your limit is the first offer that you make. It just means that when you submit your first offer, you know how far you are prepared to increase your offer before it no longer works for you.

When negotiating, we must ignore the dreaded 'no'. Too many amateur negotiators hear the word no, and think that it means they can't strike a deal, and that no means no. Actually, in my mind, no just means tell me more. When someone says no, it's because you haven't satisfied their doubts or adequately answered questions or objections in their mind. So you have to dig deeper. Perhaps you've gone in too heavy too soon without building up enough rapport, or you haven't asked the right questions to find the real motivator. Maybe they just aren't motivated enough yet, but you know if you wait a little longer they will be.

Third party authority is a powerful tool when negotiating. The reason being, if the seller believes you are the sole decision maker and the person who will be buying the property, then they can pressure you for an offer from the first moment, which they'll attempt to do over the phone. Placing authority on a third party, outside of yourself, be it a business partner, accountability partner, mentor, or investors, allows you to be a helping hand and gives you the freedom and time to chat to them, build rapport, and work out the details. An example of this would be to say, "My business partner makes the final decisions when it comes to finance, but my role here is to get as much information as possible in order to have that conversation." This stops the seller from holding you to an exact price, and allows you more time to do your due diligence, before going back with a firm offer that you know will work for you.

Never be the first to make an offer. Once you make that offer, you can't go lower than the amount you've stated, so you'll want to be artfully vague with your figures and terms, using phrases like 'around about', and 'in the region of'. If you know your limit, lets say it's £75,000, then you'd be looking to come in lower than that. If you were being forced into making an offer, then based on your limit you'd want to say something like, "Around about £65,000." Now, from here, you know your limit and can start to negotiate up if the seller point-blank refuses. The important thing here though, is that you have your limit and you've started way below, in order to allow yourself room to negotiate the best price. If you get a yes at this point, you've negotiated a great deal for yourself. If you have to negotiate up, then at least you know your top line.

Another tactic you can use, is to go from one extreme to the other. If for example, you asked a seller, "How much under £100,000 would you be willing to accept?" then chances are you won't get any of them to think of a figure below £95,000. They're not going to negotiate with themselves, so they'll stay as close to the £100,000 as possible. Instead, we flip this around to the other extreme, and ask "How much above the £65,000 would you be willing to accept?" By doing this, they'll still want more than £65,000, but they might answer with a figure such as, "Around about £80,000." Just by changing the question, you've automatically pulled the seller down. The psychology around this makes it feel unreasonable to go from £65,000 to £100,000, whereas the other way around, will do you more harm than good.

Justify your every move.

Justify what you're doing and why you're doing it. You'll want to bring closure to the seller's mind instead of having them wonder things like, "Why is the offer only that amount?" If you justify your every move then you'll explain to them why the offer is what it is. "In order to establish a quick sale", "Because the investor is a cash buyer", or "Because of the costs associated with the renovation work". So, the seller then starts to piece this together and feels comfortable because you've explained and justified everything to them. You've left them with no doubt that this is the right way forward.

Remember, questions are the answers. Do not steamroll the conversation. Instead, ask quality questions and listen to their answers. Be sincere in your approach and take a genuine interest. By doing so, you'll naturally put them at ease and let them know you have their best interests at heart.

As we wrap up this chapter, hopefully you're starting to get a feel for what has been a taste of the strategies and tactics available for negotiating with sellers in order to establish win-win outcomes. At Property

Protege ™, we dig deep into our entire armoury of golden rules for negotiation, and give you an experience of negotiating in a live environment, which is always fun. But for now, I hope you've taken some strong lessons away from this chapter, and I hope everything thus far is making sense.

BONUS CONTENT

Visit YourPropertyJumpstart.com/bonus
for your secret bonus chapter, the Protege Deal Calculator,
and additional content and resources to support you
on your property journey

CHAPTER 11:
CREATING YOUR WAR PLAN

I'm impressed.

Unless you skipped ahead to this point, you've made it.

You've officially reached the very final section of *Your Property Jumpstart* ™.

And what a journey it's been...

We've covered the property millionaire mindset, the foundations and fundamentals, due diligence, mastering our Goldmine Area, various long-term and short-term investment strategies, raising finance, joint ventures, deal sourcing, and negotiation.

Correct me if I'm wrong, but you literally have before you the full package to go out and build a five or six or seven-figure property business, and there's only one person who can stop you.

In this final chapter of the book, let's discuss your war plan; essentially ticking the right boxes and lining up everything we've covered thus far, to prepare you to go to war. Let's bring it all home.

TREAT IT AS A BUSINESS

First and foremost, you must treat your property business, as a business. If you treat it as a hobby or a pastime, you'll get hobby income. If you treat it as a business, even if you're only operating for one hour per day, you'll get matching results, as a business owner. Most people receive a shock when they enter the world of self-employment, and even if you're still working full-time and starting your property business on the side, you're still entering the realms of self-employment. The difficulty with this, is that you're the boss. It's easy to work when the boss is watching, but what happens when you have no one there to hold you accountable, to tell you to step it up, to nudge you when they know you have more in you, to kick start motivation when all you feel like doing is resting after a long day in your current job. It's not easy, but you simply have to put one foot in front of the other, and refuse to settle for less than you can be. If you're working for one hour, give your absolute maximum to that hour. Take the right actions, in the time you work.

FOCUS FOCUS FOCUS

Like in any business, you have to have clarity and focus. You don't start a fire with a magnifying glass by continually moving the glass. You must hold it in one position. We've shared a handful of powerful strategies, we've spoken about buy-to-let, we've spoken about buy-to-flip, and we've spoken about packaging deals. There's been a great deal covered in this book, but when it comes to clarity and focus, it's time to knuckle down, determine how you're going to approach your property business to get some cashflow behind you, and then aggressively pursue that course of action. Don't attempt to focus on everything. Focus on one or two things, and complimentary add-ons where appropriate. Be strict with yourself. Avoid those shiny objects. Know your outcome and get after it. As a starting point, I'm going to recommend you put in a minimum of 10 hours per week on your property business. However, the more hours you can put in, the more you're going to get back. And the more you put in, the faster you'll give yourself the freedom of choice in whether or not to go full-time in property.

MASTER YOUR GOLDMINE AREA

We've discussed it at length. It's been brought up several times. Now it's time to determine your Goldmine Area and choose to master it. Where do you want to focus in terms of being the local expert and authority? Where do you want to focus your marketing and dominate the game? Again, with clarity and focus comes results. As we've discussed, your Goldmine Area should be a few miles radius, and each day, you should be seeking to further understand that market. What are the local property values? What type of properties are there? What kind of rents could you achieve? Get to know and understand and master your target area. Once you've built your skillset, you'll be in a great position to begin to look at other markets if you choose. To get yourself started, and to get multiple deals under your belt, choose your area, now.

CRAFT YOUR MARKETING PLAN

Here's my advice. Go and review the entire chapter on property sourcing. Why? Because your job is to source the deals and raise the finance. Go and review the chapter, get your website and other materials up and running, and start bringing in the business. You may feel the temptation to procrastinate on this, wondering if you should get your knowledge up to scratch first. The answer is no. Just go for it. It's better to have business coming in and learning as you go, than having great knowledge, but no business coming in.

If you don't have funds to invest in marketing, even though your startup costs will be minimal, you can of course tap into various strategies and put yourself out there, but just how fast do you want to make money and start to build your business? As with anything, you find the resources to make it happen, and you weigh it up against the upside return. The more money you make, the more you funnel into your marketing. Dominate the game. Remember, this is property. This is awesome. There's a world of opportunity and potential on your doorstep, but you have to make the moves and bring it home.

BUILD YOUR PROPERTY POWER TEAM

Early in *Your Property Jumpstart* ™, we discussed the importance of building your Property Power Team. Don't be phased by this. You need to start identifying each of the people you'll need for your power team. Then, speak to them, interview them essentially, ask them questions, find out what they're involved in, and get a feel for them. Don't go in with your tail between your legs like they're the professional and you're a little newbie.

No, go in like a boss, because you're making this shit happen, and you're finding the right people to back you and work with.

TAP INTO MULTIPLE STREAMS OF PROPERTY INCOME

The most important aspect of property is not the bolt-ons, but the strategies themselves. With that being said, once you're moving with the various strategies, make sure you scrub-up and get to grips with the cashflow strategies as well as leveraging your power team for additional income. There are many ways to generate revenue in property, and any additional income you do bring in should come as a complement to activities you're already doing. Do yourself a favour and cut any 'scammy', 'spammy', or 'fly-by-night' little earners you're hanging onto. Let's make some real money. As well as focusing on short-term cashflow strategies and tapping into your power team for additional income, start raising finance. Write down all of the people you know that tick the boxes of the points we covered in the raising finance module. Become the kind of person you have to be, upgrade your life and attitude, and get out there and start educating other people on what it is that you know to get joint venture partners. You always want to look for ways of raising finance because the last thing that you want is to be left with no money, while the funds you have raised or gained access to are out to work, and you're twiddling your fingers, waiting to see what's going to happen. When the next deal comes, make sure you have funds to act on it.

10X YOUR RESULTS

I'm going to recommend one book other than this one, for now. Go and purchase **Grant Cardone's 'The 10X Rule'**.

You want to 10X everything you're doing. Perhaps you're planning on doing 10 viewings, great, go and do 100 over the same time period. The more viewings you do, the more familiar you'll become with your Goldmine Area and the people and properties in it. You'll better understand renovation costs, what walk-in condition looks like, and so on. This is just one example. You should be 10X'ing across the board. Whatever you're doing, assume that it's going to take ten times more effort, ten times more work, and ten times the resources and mindset you're bringing to the table. Go in armed and ready for war.

PURSUE AND ACHIEVE FINANCIAL FREEDOM

Have you identified your financial freedom figure? Have you made a list of all of your expenses, and everything you have to have covered in a given month? Once you know what it's going to take to cover your bases, you have your freedom figure. Now, are you prepared to make the short-term sacrifices, cut back on your spending, and do the work to make it happen? Many people will attempt to build a buy-to-let portfolio in order to create the financial freedom to leave full-time employment and pursue a full-time property business. However, as you hopefully grasp by now, that's going to take some time. There are other ways of looking at this. For example, now that you know your minimum level figure, you basically now know what you have to achieve each month to make it happen. So, how about proving to yourself that you can produce at least one packaged deal that equals or exceeds your monthly figure? Will that give you the confidence to go full-time? Or will it give you the confidence to borrow 3-6 months worth of bill money, in order to aggressively pursue your property business and get the deals flowing? The point is, identify your number. I used to think I'd have to be raking in tens of thousands in order to achieve financial freedom, before someone pointed out that all I really needed was a couple of thousand per month, which would give me the starting block to go out and create real wealth with the benefit of full-time hours.

You owe it to yourself to become financially free, to give yourself what most people crave in life: choices and options. With financial freedom comes choice; the choice to go full-time with property as your main focus, the choice to work your own hours, the choice to increase the quality of your lifestyle, and the choice to say no to things that you couldn't say no to before. There is no better feeling than living life on your own terms.

Not only do you owe it to yourself to become financially free, you owe it to others too; those who will look at the results you have achieved and see the life you now live. They'll see you living life on your own terms, doing what you want, when you want, and wherever you want. You will become an inspiration for those closest to you; inspiring them into taking action to go out and pursue their own dreams. It will become much more real to them that someone they know has made it out of the rat race and is doing well for themselves.

Going one step further, you owe it to people you haven't even met yet, to become financially free. I never thought for one minute that I would cause such a profound ripple effect to the magnitude that I have created by being that beacon of hope and inspiration to tens of thousands of people. If I hadn't ruthlessly pursued my dreams and did whatever it took to become financially free, I wouldn't have impacted those closest to me at the early stages of my journey and I wouldn't have inspired thousands of people I've yet to meet who have listened to my podcasts, and saw me speak at events across the country. Then there are those who have gone through our Property Protege ™ programme. And now *you* too, reading this book. You too, can be that person, who inspires and motivates more people than you could possibly imagine by achieving the first step of financial freedom.

DEVELOP YOUR PROPERTY MILLIONAIRE MINDSET

We kicked off this book with the Property Millionaire Mindset. I'd suggest you review that chapter when times get tough, and when things aren't going your way. For example, when your offers are being rejected, when you reach the final hurdle and a sale falls through, when you have tenant problems, when you have issues with renovations, issues with contractors, and a whole host of other challenges. It's going to happen. I can assure you of that. Don't let it get you down. This is the game you've signed up for. Every business and every profession has its challenges. Embrace it, and actively get better in the game. The Property Millionaire Mindset chapter will give you that lift and the reminders you need to get back on track.

COMMIT TO STRATEGIC LEARNING

Sometimes, people who've attended Property Protege ™ will ask me, "Paul, as part of my morning study, what books should I read?" My answer, is of course, "Have you mastered the content in the online Protege Vault?" I already know the answer. Why learn more, when you haven't mastered what you've already learned? Some people will tell you to read 100 good books. I'd suggest you read one or two good books 100 times. When people come onto Property Protege ™, I tell them to master the content in our online Protege Vault, until it becomes second nature, and part of who they are. Here and now, I'm telling you to do the same with this book. Don't go and read 20 other property training books. Master this one. Or, if you don't like me or my approach, bin this one, and go find a mentor that you resonate with. The point is, find someone who has walked the path before you, learn from them, master what you learn, and then aggressively pursue it. On that note, aside from mastering the content in this book, and hopefully Property Protege ™ if you choose to apply, the only other content I'd recommend you tap into, is that which raises your mindset. Of course, you have the Millionaire Mindset chapter in this book, and you have the vast content in the online Protege Vault if you join Property Protege ™, all of which you should master. But above and beyond this, if you happen to find yourself listening to podcasts or audiobooks, make sure it's content that lifts your standard of living, and lifts your internal game and capacity.

JOIN US ON PROPERTY PROTEGE ™

In this book, I've given you a complete war map. I've held nothing back at this level. You could take what you've learned here and put it to work to build a six or seven-figure business.

With that being said…

Why not give yourself the gift of acceleration?

Why not tap into high-level mentorship and accountability?

Why not tap into more thorough and comprehensive training on what you've learned?

Why not tap into a community of like-minded people, many of whom are on the same journey, and many of whom are much further down the path and only too willing to help show you the way? You never know, you may just find your next joint venture partner in there.

Why not tap into a ready-made power team?

Why not tap into weekly accountability and group sessions to stay on track?

Why not tap into a support network where every question you'll have will be answered?

If you truly want this, and what you've learned in this book has been enough to show you what's possible, then why not ensure success and give yourself every opportunity to make it happen?

We have one core programme: Property Protege ™.

Property Protege ™ is the absolute top level when it comes to property education in the UK. We've been playing this game aggressively since 2006, and have a wealth of real-world knowledge, experience, and a proven track record of results. We're a deal-doing company first, and an education company second, which gives us the best opportunity to provide the highest level real-time education to our mentees. We've taken all sorts of people from all walks of life, both new and experienced, from across the UK, and also internationally, and turned them into successful, high-performance property professionals.

Property Protege ™ is the beginning, the middle, and the end. Nothing is left out. Everything is given. Whether you want to go full-time in the fastest time possible, create a six-figure income, build a seven-figure portfolio, replace your pension, or even supplement your existing income alongside your current career, we can walk you through it.

If you're serious about success in property, then give yourself this gift and opportunity.

To find out more and apply for Property Protege ™, visit **propertyprotege.com** and click the application button. You'll fill in a short form to share a little background with us. You'll then be given a link to schedule a call with a member of our team. On the call, we will have a conversation to answer your questions, find out a little more about you, find out what you want to achieve, and ensure that Property Protege ™ is the right fit for you. All going well, we'll discuss the investment with you, and welcome you aboard, and then the process of turning your desires into reality will begin.

Visit **propertyprotege.com** to find out more.

LET'S GO TO WAR

So, we've made it.

It's been an intense process, but you're here.

I want to congratulate you for getting to this point.

Most people who pick up a book like this barely make it past the first few chapters.

The very fact that you've made it to this point tells me that you're different, that you truly want this, and that providing you apply yourself and what you've learned, you'll make it happen.

You now have the tools and knowledge to change your life.

So what are you going to do about it?

There's only one thing to do.

LET'S GO TO WAR!

Let's take action. Let's make it happen.

Master your mindset. Master the content. Do not stop until you get there.

Hopefully our paths will cross, be that at some point down the line, or be that at Property Protege ™, should you choose to invest in yourself and in your accelerated success.

Until we next meet, I wish you good health and good luck.

I hope everything you've been looking for comes to pass.

Please, give yourself this gift. I look forward to hearing your story.

Yours sincerely,
Paul McFadden

PROPERTY PROTEGE ™

To learn more about Property Protege ™ and to hear from many of the people who have already attended, go to:

propertyprotege.com

ABOUT THE AUTHOR

Paul McFadden is a renowned and respected high-performance, property, and business success coach.

As a successful entrepreneur and authority on wealth creation, Paul's ongoing mission and commitment is in supporting others in developing their own wealth through property and business.

After a difficult start in life, growing up in a single parent household with little to no financial resources, Paul discovered that a lack of resources, was less important than an attitude of resourcefulness, coupled with a strong mindset of possibility and good old hard work.

From a standing start, with no funds, no experience, and no track record, Paul built a multi-million pound property portfolio, bought and flipped millions of pounds worth of property, and has packaged over £250 million worth of property investments, as well as being responsible for helping countless others, including many prominent and well known people in the property industry, become full time property investors.

Whether through Paul's free resources online, or by helping you transform your fortunes in property and business through coaching, training or mentoring, Paul hopes to help you live a full expression of yourself, and discover your own power and capabilities.

paulmcfaddenwealth.com

paulmcfaddenwealth.com

Printed in Great Britain
by Amazon